EAT YOUR WAY TO THE TOP

31 Habits for Optimising
Your Potential
at Work and Beyond

Angela Steel

Eat your Way to the Top –
31 Habits for Optimising Your Potential at Work and Beyond

This edition first published by SuperWellness Publishing,
431 London Road,
Cheam SM3 8JN, UK
Email: angela@superwellness.co.uk

Cover and text design by ebook-designs.co.uk

A CIP record for this book is available from the British Library.

ISBN 978-0-9574131-2-2

Dedication:

For John

Contents

Acknowledgements

Going back to where it all began, I thank my parents, Carol and Gerry, for instilling in me a love of real food from a young age. Growing up eating freshly grown vegetables straight from the garden is a rare privilege I wish more people could enjoy.

My thanks go to all who have encouraged me and supported me along the way: Gilian Crowther for sharing so much knowledge in such a selfless way, and for her feedback and advice with this book, and the other inspiring members of the Academy of Nutritional Medicine. Thanks to Teresa Dupay, Tricia Jones, Tarnia Nebbitt, Andy Wright, Arthur Partridge, Dean Hughes, Jenni Henderson, Dave Sharpe, Shermine Boustany, Pierre Croset and Nollaig Griffin. Thanks to Dr Tahir Masood for introducing me to a new and powerful exercise paradigm that has transformed the work I do. Thanks also to Professor Basant Puri for writing such a wonderful foreword to this book.

My appreciation goes to my corporate clients who have supported the birth and development of the SuperWellness nutrition challenge and other corporate work: Kate and Kaye at Blue Apple for putting my recipes to the test, Derek Jones at Kuoni, Emma Cutbill at Incisive Media, Susanne Sucka at Harrods and all the challenge participants who have been so inspiring and good fun to work with. Thanks to those who have inspired and mentored me: Peter

Thomson, Daniel Priestley, Alicia Dunhams, Dr Richard Wetherby and especially Esther O'Halloran for galvanising me into finishing this book after much procrastination. Thanks to Antony Hepworth for his smashing design work. I also send huge thanks to my private clients from whom I've learnt so much.

Thank you to my sister Cathy for all her support and interest throughout. They mean a lot. And finally of course thanks to my partner John for his considerable patience, belief and support. Without you none of this would be even possible.

Foreword

I t gives me great pleasure to contribute the foreword to Eat Your Way to the Top: 31 Habits for Optimising Your Potential at Work and Beyond. The author, Angela Steel MA, NT Dip, CNHC reg (Naturopathy), is a highly knowledgeable and successful naturopathic nutritional therapist and corporate wellness expert who has previously authored a seven-step dynamic weight loss and high energy system.

In her latest work, Angela again utilises up-to-date evidence-based scientific information to show how one's potential at work (and outside of work) can be optimised through proper nutrition. Not only is this book well researched, but full scientific references are given, which will enable the reader to check the original source material; many of the scientific papers have been published since 2010. Having said that, I should not like to give the impression that this book has the turgid quality of some scientific texts. On the contrary, it is highly enjoyable and easy to read. It is well illustrated and contains many informative case histories and 'myth alerts'. Reading the book is rather like attending several riveting lectures. There are also links to the author's web site.

Chapters 3 to 7 (inclusive) furnish the reader with practical weekly plans. These carefully guide the reader week by week. They will help the busy professional (or student) in numerous ways, from how to choose optimum meals at home or when staying in a hotel, to coping with the additional pressures of travelling and rushing to meetings. Following this guidance will be rather like having one's own life coach – at a fraction of the price.

In all, 31 habits are explained for optimisation of one's potential. These are not all purely nutritional in nature. They also, for example, include advice regarding sleep and detoxing. Angela also includes a brilliant recipe selection which features mouth-watering photographs of delicious and nutritious meals.

In sum, I am delighted to recommend this work very highly indeed.

Professor B. K. Puri
London

Prof. Basant Puri, MA (Cantab), PhD, MB, BChir, BSc (Hons) MathSci, DipStat, PG Cert Maths, MMath, FRCPsych, FSB is based at Hammersmith Hospital, Imperial College London, Breakspear Clinic, UL and UPN, as both a medical practitioner and a researcher. His research involves biochemical and state-of-the-art electrophysiological and brain scanning techniques.

Introduction

" Successful people form habits that feed their success, instead of habits that feed their failure."
Jeff Olson

In the competitive world we live in, better performance, whether it means more creative ideas, greater energy or a sharper mind, is what creates success. No wonder millions of pounds are spent each year on self-development books and coaching programmes! But what about our biochemical success factors? It's not just athletes who benefit from optimising their diet. Anyone who doesn't seriously consider using nutrition to their advantage has to be missing a trick.

Indeed, most people don't realise it, but what they choose to eat and drink each day has a powerful influence on their health *and* on what they achieve in life. In fact, a recent study led by Brigham Young University concluded that the impact diet has on work performance and productivity is as high as *66%*. Imagine what a difference a 10% improvement in productivity would have on your life, let alone 66%!

And it's not just that good nutrition can give you the edge, but surely the wellbeing it creates should in itself be seen as an integral part of success! As Arianna Huffington, co-founder and Editor in Chief of Huffington Post found out herself: "If we don't redefine what success is, the price we pay in terms of our health and well-being will continue to rise [...] We are entering a new era. How we measure success is changing."

Whether you're considering the success of your own life and career, or as an employer, the success of your business, which depends on the people you employ, nutrition is a topic that can give you the edge, but can also seriously undermine you if you ignore its importance. With 50% of the UK population predicted by become obese by 2050 (according to the Foresight Report: Tackling Obesities, Future Choices, 2007), the burden of nutrition related disease is set to increase. According to 2014 figures by Diabetes UK, the number of people with diabetes has doubled since 1996 and the number of obesity related hospital admissions has increased ten-fold in ten years. This means that we are all potentially affected as individuals, and the costs to each and every business is most certainly increasing.

And yet all of these outcomes can be modified by behaviour. So how does one tap into this wasted potential, and put nutrition into practice without a full time chef and coach by their side? Not to mention coping with business trips, vending machines and biscuit pushing colleagues?

The aim of this book is to provide practical and inspiring answers to these questions, and an easy to follow methodology to help high achieving professionals reach the top of their game, in a way that fits with the demands of a busy life.

HOW IT BEGAN FOR ME

Until January 2007, I was only vaguely aware of a discipline called nutrition. It was only my appetite for personal development and new experiences, which opened that door for me. Fascinated by a very graphic article I'd read in the Saturday Guardian, depicting the journalist's experience of doing a fasting detox in Thailand (with full-page photos of all the colonic waste which had resulted!) I decided to complete a seven day fast in Phuket, at a detox retreat that year. My work colleagues in the IT company I worked for at the time thought it was a weird choice. Not their idea of fun, that's for sure.

And they were certainly right in some respects. The detox effect was powerful and I spent a good part of my holiday in bed, feeling atrocious. However, after a couple of days readapting to 'normal food', the feeling of wellbeing I had was unequalled. I had a sense of clarity and a level of inspiration I didn't even know was possible. The only way I can describe it is 'concentrated vitality'. I'd wake up at 5am, full of energy and in high spirits, get to the office, actually *excited* about the day ahead and just plough through my tasks, accomplishing in a day what would normally take a week. Everything seemed easier and within my reach – my positivity radiated, and boosted my confidence, which had great knock on effects in meetings and my interactions with other people. For a few weeks, it's almost as if I felt invincible, and I wanted to feel this way for ever.

Unfortunately, as I returned to my work routine, the feeling gradually wore off. So what was my work routine? It might sound familiar to you. A long commute (an hour and a half each way), which took me through Waterloo station, with all its coffee vendors, hence a daily cappuccino! A business park with its limited selection of food on offer - a burger van affectionately known as 'Dirty Barry's', a Harvester pub next door, and a sandwich van that called around 11am, with a selection of egg sandwiches, buns and cheese straws. And the kitchen, where some of us would get together for lunch.

I didn't lose sight of what was possible. I knew that the tiredness that was creeping back in was not inevitable. It wasn't a 'sleep' problem. I was waking up exhausted after hours of sleep. You might have experienced this too? It seemed obvious to me that this was very much connected to what I ate and drank every day. I was determined to recapture that memorable feeling I'd had for a couple of weeks after my fasting holiday. If only I was able to feel that way as a 'norm' then I would be able to achieve so much more. I wouldn't waste so much time staring at my screen trying to work up the motivation to think clearly. I would be able to concentrate on the task at hand and get results faster. Get the energy and drive I needed to complete what I undertook – effortlessly. And I would be jumping out of bed each morning, ready to take on any task, even after a long train journey.

The detox had given me a taste of what was possible, but I wasn't about to start fasting on a regular basis at home. What I needed now was a practical way to achieve this level of wellbeing through my everyday habits.

GRADUAL STEPS

I started a part-time study course in nutrition, and began to gradually make changes to my way of eating. I won't pretend this was from one extreme to the other – I was never a junk food fan. I had always been fairly health conscious. In fact, I would never have previously considered my diet might need changing in any way. How wrong I'd been! I was finding out that many of the foods I took for granted as healthy were in fact doing me a disservice. I was introducing new foods that I now knew to be packed with nutrition and goodness, and little by little, the benefits came.

The most visible sign of improvement was my skin. Acne had always been the bane of my life, even as an adult in my early thirties. Finally, for the first time, it was beginning to clear up and I started to feel much more confident as a result. Can you imagine how good that felt? It began to shift my self-image. In my mind's eye I'd always pictured myself with acne, prompting a sickening feeling of shame. Now my complexion was acquiring a 'glow' that I'd never imagined possible.

As time went on, and as I noticed more clearly how food affected me, my diet became more and more fine-tuned to my body's needs. It didn't happen overnight.

NUTRITION AT WORK

Throughout my earlier journey of discovery with nutrition, when I was studying and going through the steepest learning curve, I worked in an office environment.

Like many of my fellow 9-5ers (and anyone spending half of their waking hours or more at work), I had always been on the lookout for convenience foods that wouldn't take too long to prepare or eat. Does this sound familiar? I remember feeling I had 'nailed' breakfast with wholesome looking cereal bars I could carry in my bag and eat on the crowded train on my way into work, even if I was standing up!

I thought of myself as a 'healthy eater' and as such was a prime target for food marketers beating the 'health' drum. I felt a glow of good conscience each time I filled my trolley with little yogurt pots that purported to be 'good for my intestinal flora'. I made a beeline for the fruit juice, a great source of vitamin C I thought. Little did I know that those benefits were far outweighed by their sugar and fructose content! It didn't even cross my mind to question some foods that had always been such a staple part of my diet then (like tomato ketchup, a savoury sauce containing 25% sugar).

I had been only too happy to fit in with office eating and drinking rituals. Binge drinking on white wine and then recovering from the hangover of a work night out by stopping at the burger van for a bacon roll. These things were *the norm* and I never used to question them. They even gave me a sense of belonging, of being part of a fun culture. I wouldn't have wanted to be excluded from that.

And then as I began to make my nutrition discoveries, I started to think more independently. I could see what these habits were doing to me and I felt less and less the need to conform. My lunches began to stand out slightly, often featuring unusual ingredients like quinoa or sprouted seeds and I got used to quizzical looks and exclamations of 'that looks healthy!' The banter was always good-natured and I was quite happy by then to be seen as a 'non conformist'. This was an amazing development for my self-confidence and the feeling I was living by my own beliefs, not just taking on behaviours in order to fit in.

What I struggled with most was my own judgement of others' habits. With the zeal of the newly converted, I was keen for everyone else to realise the error of their ways. I desperately wanted them to ditch the sugar and preservative laden sauces and toxic treats from the snack machine. I bit my lip when one of my friends, run down and fed up with catching virus after virus, nipped out at lunch to buy herself a giant bag of Maltesers as a treat. I wished she'd known that the sugar was going to weaken her immune system further and stop her feeling better. I felt disapproving and judgmental, and sometimes quite isolated.

Thankfully I eventually learnt to let go of the wish to 'convert' everyone to healthy eating and accept that it wasn't top of everyone's priority list! What I did notice however, was that knowledge is a powerful motivator once people have access to it. Hence I developed the firm belief that 'real' information about nutrition had to become accessible to more people, and that became my purpose. It led me to change my career, becoming a nutritional therapist, first working with individuals, and then gradually moving into corporate wellness.

EMPOWERED TO IMPROVE
What I realised was that work was often the biggest challenge people had to deal with. The lack of time, the need for convenience, the pull of work culture and peer pressure.

And at the same time, these pressures were causing adverse health effects, which had repercussions in their personal and professional lives. Not just mild tiredness and the odd day off for ill health, but in some cases, major problems that directly impinged on their performance at work. Severe fatigue, or embarrassing digestive conditions could make work a dreaded place to be, even causing people to reduce their working hours. I realised I could draw on my own experiences to help them get a better understanding of nutrition, but also put it into practice wherever they worked, in a way that was not extreme or isolating. You might have been there

– wanting to make changes, but afraid that new habits might set you apart and make it difficult to 'fit in'.

Everyone is entitled to make their own choices, but without reliable information, this idea is just a myth. People's choices will be made for them by food advertisers, industry lobbies that influence government policies and peer pressure from their friends, families and colleagues. Like many of the clients I've worked with over the years, you may have experienced the frustration of reading or hearing conflicting advice. Unsure which way to go, you might have just been tempted to give up trying!

This book is the result of what I've discovered, from working with hundreds of clients in the workplace and piecing together the 'formula' which led to the best results, in terms of health, energy and performance.

The 'Eat Your Way To The Top' Formula

NUTRITION: AN UNTAPPED TOOL FOR SELF-DEVELOPMENT

If you're the kind of person who's driven to achieve at work, self-development is probably high up on your priority list. You've probably invested time, energy and money in training, mentoring or coaching throughout your career. You might not have given too much thought to what you eat and drink as another method for increasing your success at work. And yet, what proportion of your hard-won skills and ability are being undermined by physical states of discomfort or fatigue?

Have you thought how much potential you're wasting when all you feel like doing is resting your head on the desk and going to sleep for an hour or so after lunch - every day? When you find yourself reading the same paragraph for the fourth time and struggling to take it in properly? When you get that sneaking feeling that your daily habits are gradually undermining your health? These are the immeasurable, insidious gremlins that erode your effectiveness. And the beginning of a vicious cycle that threatens your quality of life at work and in your personal life too: see figure 1.

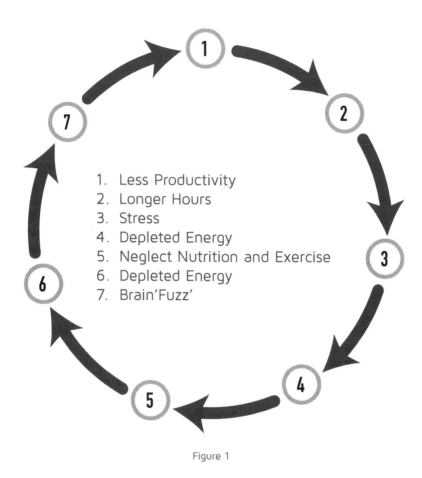

1. Less Productivity
2. Longer Hours
3. Stress
4. Depleted Energy
5. Neglect Nutrition and Exercise
6. Depleted Energy
7. Brain 'Fuzz'

Figure 1

As you grab a quick sandwich, not wishing to 'eat' into your work time, your work time expands to include the post-carbohydrate dip in energy that inevitably follows. And what you eat and drink doesn't just affect your energy levels, it has an impact on your motivation, your clarity of thinking, your mood, your quality of sleep and your ability to cope with stress. Wouldn't it be useful to improve your performance in all of these areas? Just imagine what the results might be, in 6 months time, a year, 5 years or 10 years down the line if you did...

How can you do this?

There is a formula. It's an approach which I've seen work consistently with the professionals and business owners I've coached over the years. But before I explain how it works, let's have a look at why eating well at work is a challenge for so many people. And hopefully you'll realise that the things that get in the way for you are the same as they are for everyone else too. Step by step, it's possible to work adjustments into your routine and the pay-off will be worth it a thousand times over.

WHY EATING WELL AT WORK CAN BE CHALLENGING

You're probably all too familiar with the reasons why... Let's face it, most work environments are not designed with healthy eating in mind. Good food is often not readily available and there might not even be a facility to store your own. My first job, on the outskirts of London was in an office on an industrial park, and there was not much choice, other than greasy spoons for miles around. Without a kitchen or a fridge for storing my own food, it certainly was a challenge, not that all those years ago, I was especially aware of it being an issue – luckily perhaps!

When you're in a work situation, you're often not in control of the choices available to you. The sandwiches served at a client meeting, the lunch from the service station, which is the only option on your way to see a client, the limited selection of snacks served at the cafeteria. Not to mention that each workplace has its own rituals, which can be hard to avoid if you want to 'fit in'. Socialising, celebrating and bonding often revolve around food and drink.

And then there's the four-letter word: TIME! Sometimes sleep seems like a luxury when there is so much to do... Let alone spending much time thinking about what to eat. This is probably why eating is something which tends to be done at the same time as other activities: swallowing a sandwich while checking emails, gulping down some breakfast on the train, grabbing a bite while rushing out of the door. And time *is* a precious commodity. Whatever you do for food when your days are so manically packed with activity will have to be very efficient indeed.

No wonder convenience has become the priority when making food choices. This is why cereals became so popular, and then to avoid the 'lengthy' process of putting cornflakes in a bowl and pouring milk over them, cereal bars! Work pressure is not going to go away, so food does have to be convenient. However not at the cost of your energy and long-term health, otherwise in the long term, it becomes rather inconvenient!

I'm not saying it's easy. Our work life can be all consuming. Whether you are an employee or an entrepreneur working from home, whether your workplace is an office, a shop, your car or multiple hotels, your eating and drinking habits will have been to some extent shaped by your work. And in turn be deciding the shape of things to come, your health outlook, your enjoyment of life and yes, the results you get too. Just to close the circle.

What those habits are costing you is something only you can gauge. And whether you are worth the effort to change is something for you alone to decide. If you are prepared to let go of some habits and even some old beliefs, and embrace a new way, then yes, you can change your life with nutrition.

HOW THIS BOOK IS STRUCTURED TO
EMPOWER YOU WITH THE 'FORMULA'

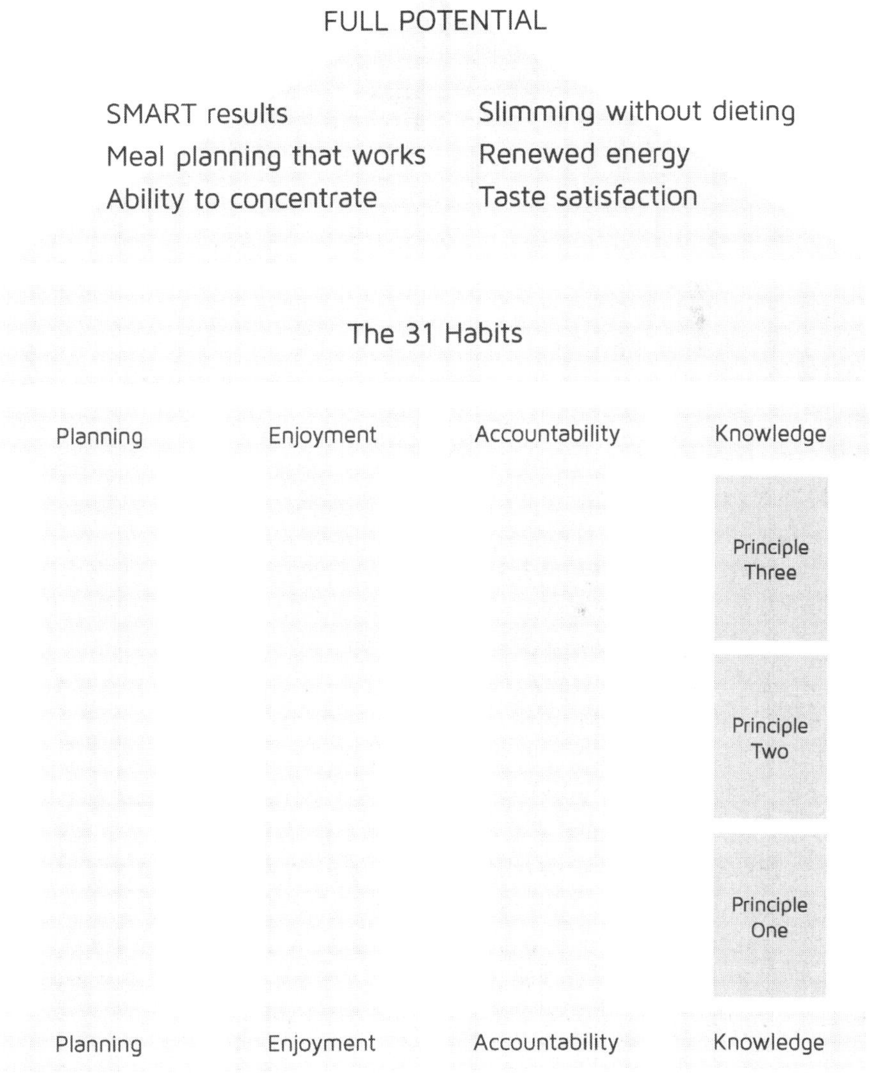

FULL POTENTIAL

SMART results   Slimming without dieting
Meal planning that works   Renewed energy
Ability to concentrate   Taste satisfaction

The 31 Habits

Planning	Enjoyment	Accountability	Knowledge
			Principle Three
			Principle Two
			Principle One
Planning	Enjoyment	Accountability	Knowledge

Figure 2

Over the years, I've repeated many times the same advice to my clients in private consultations and in my seminars. I've often felt frustrated that I was only able to pass on this information to one person or a limited group of people at once. My goal, in writing this book, has been to gather in one place this information, and the practical advice that goes with it, which consistently achieves life-changing results.

Here's what you need to successfully apply the formula for yourself:

1. P.E.A.K. Foundation – the four pillars, including planning, enjoyment, accountability and knowledge
2. The three knowledge principles
3. The 31 habits that will transform your eating habits and the results you get, one step at a time.

I'll talk about the P.E.A.K. Foundation in this introduction. Chapter 1 will be all about the three principles of health and nutrition that make up the 'Knowledge' pillar:

- Nourishing the body with nutrient dense foods
- Balancing the metabolism with a low glycaemic load diet
- Optimising digestive function and detoxification.

Chapters 3, 4, 5, 6 and 7 describe the 31 habits, divided into five weeks (one per chapter, following specific themes). Practising these habits one at a time will get you closer to the SMART results listed below (and the ability to reach your full potential):

Slimming without dieting
Meal planning that works
Ability to concentrate
Renewed energy
Taste satisfaction

Following the 31 habits, you'll find over 20 recipes, all tried and tested by many of my clients over the years. They are firm favourites, which I hope you will adopt into your weekly repertoire too, providing you with ideas that you can put into practice easily, quickly and with excellent results.

The key to success, in my experience, is to approach this as a step-by-step process, not putting too much pressure on yourself to make changes faster than you're comfortable with. Motivation is not something that can be forced (certainly for no longer than a brief amount of time). If you nurture it however, by seeking inspiration and eye-opening information, then it just takes on a life of its own, carrying you towards your goals.

Of course, I'd be lying if I were to say it was an effortless process. It still takes effort to overcome old habits, and sometimes you may take a step back. Setbacks are a normal and healthy part of any change process. The secret is not to mistake them for failure (leading you to give up). The important thing is to *just keep going*, doing what you can at the pace you can manage, and the rewards you get (more energy, less bloating, fitting into your clothes better and feeling more confident about yourself...) is what will keep pushing you to take the next step forward.

There are four pillars that you will need to put in place to make the process a lot smoother.

P.E.A.K. : THE FOUR PILLARS OF POSITIVE TRANSFORMATION

Here's the thing: nutrition is a discipline that can give you the edge, just as it does for athletes and sports professionals. In fact, if it's an area you've been neglecting, then this is probably where you stand to make your biggest win. Your underlying greatness is just about to be magnified by a massive boost to your physical and mental state!

So where do you start?

There are four pillars you need to have in place in order to begin the transformation, and I refer to them meaningfully as P.E.A.K. Here's what they are:

- Planning
- Enjoyment
- Accountability
- Knowledge

Let me explain what each of these means and why it's so important:

1. **Planning:** without planning, any change you try to introduce in your diet is usually doomed to be short-lived. We spend on average half of our waking hours at work (and you might be reading this thinking it's much longer in your case!), most of the rest goes on chores, commuting, family duties... leaving very little time for *you*. Trust me, the only way to overcome this is planning. A little investment in time (15 minutes) once a week saves countless moments of doubt, indecision and wasted visits to the store.

2. **Enjoyment:** forget the conditioning that tells us that 'healthy' and 'tasty' are at opposite ends of the food

spectrum. It's simply wrong. And by the end of this book, I certainly hope to have convinced you of the opposite. Let's be clear: no-one ever sticks long term to a way of eating they don't really enjoy. This is why diets simply fail (well, in 95% of cases, according to statistics)

3. **Accountability:** there is a widely held belief that it takes three weeks to shape a new habit, and something like nine months for it to become second nature (so you practise it without having to think about it). Well making it through the first three weeks takes a conscious effort, as do the following eight months or so. The willingness to make this effort would never be strong enough, without a goal in mind. You have to be accountable, whether it's to yourself or someone else, in order to stay on track.

4. **Knowledge:** discipline, planning and motivation are all pointless if the changes you're making are actually not really doing you any good. Nutrition is a subject deeply affected by vested interests – confusion seems to reign as various sides make contradictory claims. My goal with this book is to share with you the tried and tested knowledge about nutrition, which we have at this point, from scientific studies and experience with clients. Only when you access the knowledge you can trust, and begin to see results for yourself, can you have the confidence to keep making the right choices in the long term.

The last pillar in particular, knowledge, is a big challenge to overcome. The problem is, most people *think* they are knowledgeable about nutrition, when actually many deeply held beliefs are untrue (for example, the idea that 'low fat' foods are good for you). Most of the mainstream sources of information convey a range of myths about food, perpetuated just because they've been around for so long. Why would you even question them? It's only when you begin to dig deeper that you come across the actual studies, and they tell a very different story.

Thankfully, we're now seeing more and more of these 'red herrings' surface in the mainstream press, and so, outdated views will become increasingly less defendable. In recent years, we've seen the veil lifted on the old erroneous beliefs about fats. For example, we now know that in fact, saturated fats have very little to do with heart disease[1], and that cholesterol from food is not the danger it was claimed to be and eggs can safely be eaten every day[2]. Finally the simplistic (but attractive) 'low calorie' doctrine is also starting to look a bit tired and dusty as it becomes obvious that our metabolic processes are so much more complex than simply burning foods like a car burns fuel.

WHICH NUTRITION SYSTEM SHOULD YOU FOLLOW?

There are many nutrition 'movements'. One of the biggest challenges people have is knowing which one they should follow. Right now, it's all about the 'paleo diet' (eating foods that our ancestors in the stone-age would have eaten), and intermittent fasting is popular too. Then there's the vegan raw food movement, there's living foods and juicing. A few years ago, it was 'Atkins', and 'South Beach', the 'blood type diet', the 'zone diet', the 'low GI diet', now 'Dukan', and many more. Always in the background, there are also the deeply ingrained low calorie and low fat diets, which still hold sway in many people's minds. It's enough to drive anyone crazy!

Nutrition is an evolving science. Thankfully! Like any science *should* be. New schools of thought emerge all the time, some with more research to support them than others. As a nutrition practitioner, my job is to look at these approaches objectively, find out which ones work, and how people can put them into practice in everyday life.

There are, in my experience, rules which benefit everyone 99% of the time – the core tried and tested principles of 'eating well' if you like.

It's these core principles I want to share with you in this book, as well as the habits that make them practical. Our eating habits set the direction for our health. It's by adjusting these habits, phasing out unhelpful ones and introducing good ones, that great transformations are achieved.

A few years ago I worked with Tricia. She and her husband had set up their telephone answering business from scratch, and now they employ no fewer than 90 people. Highly successful, Tricia is a huge believer in personal development, and in fact, it was in the context of a business mentoring programme that I met her. We got chatting and she told me about some dreadful health problems she'd gone through in the previous few years. She now works as the Finance Director in her business and takes a very active role training and motivating her staff. She is a fun and lively person to be around so this role is very well suited to her.

She consulted with me and over a period of several months, I coached her to make a series of changes in her eating habits. These were all in keeping with her work routine, and we made sure that any food we removed from her diet was replaced with something more nutritious and even tastier. We also carried out functional tests on her digestive system and addressed the issues these highlighted. The outcome was significant. As well as physical improvements, she described how much better she felt she was performing at work: "Something happened and I felt a shift in energy, an outstanding and amazing shift. I felt alive. I started getting up early, looking forward to the day ahead. I began to get involved again, with my business, my friends and family. I can honestly say that after three lost years I felt back in the game."

You've probably experienced for yourself how much more creative and effective you can be when you're feeling on top form!

So are you ready to test it for yourself? Let's get started with a look at the three principles.

Chapter 1: The three core principles and the myths that undermine them

" Knowledge without practice is useless. Practice without knowledge is dangerous."
Confucius

I f you are someone who likes to understand 'why', then this chapter will give you the background you'll need in order to benefit from the rest of this book. What I want to do in the next few pages is explain to you the core principles of my approach, so that the advice that follows makes sense to you.

Just like the people I work with, you might be surprised by some of the content in this chapter – it might be at odds with what you had always thought to be true - not surprisingly, because many unfounded beliefs about nutrition still hold sway, even though science has long since moved on! I'll be highlighting these areas with the heading 'MYTH ALERT' and then proceeding to explain why this is.

SO WHAT'S HEALTHY EATING ANYWAY?

And right out of the starting blocks, we run into the first myth...

MYTH ALERT! – low calorie = healthy

When people think about food and health, it's often in terms of 'calories', and one of the most entrenched views on the matter is that 'low calorie = good and high calorie = bad'. It's the paradigm which much food industry marketing is based on and most government guidelines also. Surely the way to good health and to a thin body (both often being referred to interchangeably, which can be misleading) is to eat less and exercise more.

There's a bit more to it than this.

The "calorie" was indeed a cutting edge concept in the 19th-century when chemist Wilbur Olin Atwater first coined the term. He'd created a method of measuring a food's value in terms of energy, using the basic technology which was available to him at the time: by incinerating foods and working out how much energy they released. Our understanding of human metabolism has moved on quite considerably since then however. We don't incinerate our food as we eat it. The human body is much more complex.

The calories from different foods are not equal in terms of energy production, utilisation and storage. Carbohydrates, proteins and fats are metabolised in very different ways, meaning that some will give you lots of energy for longer whereas others will give you a very short burst of energy followed by cravings, energy dips and fat storage. In other words, calories are a useful basic unit to use in the lab, but are woefully inadequate when it comes to the human body.

A useful question to ask is this: once you've digested your food, what do the cells do with the different nutrients? Do they turn them into energy (and if so, how fast?), do they store them somewhere? (And if so, where?) It all depends which nutrients you've ingested of course. A plate of chips will give you a very different result from a plate of sausages (even at equal calories) and our aim is to understand how to optimise those choices.

IS IT JUST ABOUT CARBOHYDRATES, PROTEINS AND FATS?

It helps to know about carbohydrates, proteins and fats, but it's still not enough. These main groups are further broken down into many diverse building blocks. The Omega fats are very different from saturated fats. Protein is made up of numerous amino acids – eight of which we need to get from our diet to be in good health. Carbohydrates take many different forms, from glucose to starch to all important fibre, so a sugar cube and a broccoli floret both come under the 'carb' banner, but needless to say, their properties don't have much in common between them otherwise!

Carbohydrates, proteins and fats are known as macro-nutrients. Put simply, big enough generally that you can see or feel them: the starchy quality of a potato, the fibrous texture of a kale leaf, the oil oozing from a salmon steak. You can recognise the density of protein in the texture of a chicken fillet.

Beyond those of course there is the multitude of 'micro-nutrients' – the microscopic components of food called vitamins, minerals and phytonutrients (plant chemicals). The enablers, the catalysts, the active compounds without which our body could never use the macro-nutrients, produce energy and survive.

We are told that 'a balanced diet supplies all of the nutrients we need in adequate amounts', and this includes '5 fruit and vegetables a day'. Well as a guideline for public health (which these are) it's certainly a start. But many nutrition experts agree that as a guideline for *optimum* health, it falls very short of the mark. As an individual with a wish to maximise your level of wellness by optimising your diet, there is a wide margin for improvement.

WHAT'S MISSING?

Talking about the nutrients in a food is almost meaningless without mentioning the processing they've been through. Various stages of refinement can transform them beyond recognition, changing some of the qualities of the nutrients and adding preservatives and chemicals, which far from nourishing the body, weigh it down with a burden it's not designed to bear. So the quality and 'wholeness' of the nutrients matter, but even beyond this, there's another important matter: how your body interacts with these foods.

Let's suppose your food intake was carefully monitored and calibrated for all the right nutrients in all the right proportions. Do you think two people will have the same state of health, fat and muscle distribution and energy levels? Of course not. It all depends on their body's effectiveness at breaking down this food and extracting these nutrients. At carrying them to the cells to do their thing. And at dealing with the waste material thus created.

And before you jump to any conclusions, it's not necessarily just down to genetics. There are events, habits and external factors which influence your metabolism even more than genes (and even modify your genes themselves over time!). It could be that a course of antibiotics has modified your intestinal flora and changed its ability to extract nutrients from the foods you're digesting. Or that a particularly stressful period in your life has impacted your immune system, and resulted in your reacting to certain foods you never used to previously[3]. In turn such food intolerances can feed a cycle of inflammation which has an impact on many levels of health. A sugar habit over many years might have seriously impaired your ability to handle glucose, affecting both your energy levels and your ability to burn fat.

So understanding about the food by itself is not enough, there are also certain fundamental body processes which are important to know about. Optimising those, as well as the nutrients you put in, is what gives you the winning combination.

GENETICS + NUTRITION + BODY PROCESSES (E.G. DIGESTION) = OPTIMAL ENERGY, EFFORTLESS FAT BURNING, PEAK HEALTH

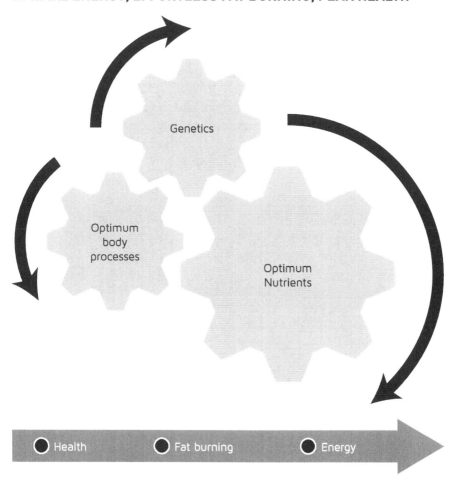

Figure 3

You're probably reading this and thinking this sounds very complex indeed. How can you optimise your nutritional choices to ensure your body has got all the raw material it needs and the best possible conditions that will give you bags of energy, effortless fat burning and the best possible health?

Let me guide you through the essentials. The approach I use with my clients is founded on three key principles:

- Feeding your body nutrient dense foods
- Balancing the metabolism with a low glycaemic load diet
- Optimising digestion and detoxification.

Let's look at each of these 3 principles in a little more detail.

1 Principle #1: Feeding your body nutrient dense foods

In our wealthy society, in which we enjoy an abundance of food, it's easy to think of malnutrition as a thing of the past. Scurvy (extreme vitamin C deficiency) and rickets (due to lack of vitamin D) might be rare occurrences, and the RDAs (recommended dietary allowances) set out by the government were calculated to avoid them. But is this good enough?

I don't think so.

There are many shades of health between life threatening deficiencies and optimum levels of wellness and I don't see why we shouldn't aim for the optimum level.

As far as plant nutrients are concerned, the 'Five a day recommended daily allowance' of fruit and vegetables is really a minimum, determined in order to avoid malnutrition ailments... it is a good goal to aim for in the first instance, but more is better if you can manage it. In fact, in the United States, the equivalent recommendation is now 9 portions of fruit and vegetables a day.

A study carried out in 1991 by McCance and Widdowson[4] showed that the nutritional content of fruit and vegetables had severely diminished since the 1940s. The researchers found that carrots contained 75% less magnesium, spinach contained 60% less iron and all fruits 27% less zinc than 50 years prior.

And it's not just vitamins and minerals from plants we need to worry about – it's also the fats which our body needs and craves, the amino acids contained in the protein we eat and the fibre which should be a big part of our diet too. And beyond the plate, let's not forget that famous nutrient we get mainly from the sun: vitamin D. I get all my clients in the UK to test their levels and over 90% are deficient. A frightening fact when vitamin D plays such a big part in preventing cancer[5].

It doesn't take much for a person to become deficient in certain nutrients. It can happen if your diet is high in 'empty calories', in other words, foods which fill the stomach without contributing much in valuable nutrients, and furthermore tax the body's nutrient bank account in order to be digested – leaving you with a negative nutrient balance. It can happen if you are vegetarian, or only eat a limited range of foods. It can also happen if you follow certain 'diets' long term. I often meet clients in my practice who have been eating 'low fat' their whole life. They often suffer from hormone imbalances, because fats provide the raw materials needed to make the hormones they need.

ANTI-NUTRIENTS

Beside the declining nutritional value of fruit and vegetables, cheap processed foods are the norm today and unfortunately tax the body without contributing many nutrients themselves. Some of these foods are fortified by the manufacturers with added nutrients, but nutrients don't work in isolation. How can artificially added nutrients ever compare with the delicate balance of nutrients - some of which we have not even yet discovered -created in nature?

For example, take this 'balanced diet' of someone who works in an office:

Morning:
50g fruit muesli with 1 cup of skimmed milk
1 cappuccino
1 cup of tea
An apple mid-morning

Lunch:
A ham and cheese brown bread sandwich
A bag of crisps
A fruit yogurt

Afternoon:
A chocolate bar
2 cups of tea

Evening:
Spaghetti bolognaise ready meal with some garlic bread and

steamed broccoli
A side salad
2 digestive biscuits and a cup of tea

How would you describe this food plan? Normal? Healthy? Balanced? Calorie wise it is on the low side (just over 2000), so it can't be that bad can it?

In fact, this way of eating is storing up problems for the future. This person's fibre intake is very deficient, even in terms of the RDA, or recommended daily allowance, which is very conservative as it is. This means possible problems with digestion in the long term. It is also very low in vitamins, minerals and plant nutrients.

Not only is it not providing enough real nutrition, it's also further weakened by the anti-nutrients it contains. In other words, foods that tax the body more than they contribute to its health. Have you spotted them?

- Sugar. This daily diet contains 110g in total - that's the equivalent of eating 20 straight teaspoons full. Just imagine what this small mountain of sugar would look like on a plate! And it's coming from the muesli (most commercial mueslis are too high in sugar, even among the ones which look 'healthy') and the dried fruit, the fruit yogurt, the chocolate bar, the ready meal (as most of these contain added sugar) and the biscuits. Not to mention the sugar which the processed carbohydrates such as bread and crisps will break down into. We're assuming the cappuccino and tea don't have added sugar.

- Caffeine, which is known to interfere with our ability to absorb iron[6] as well as vitamin D and Calcium.

- E-numbers and chemicals from the chocolate bar and the ready meal

SO WHAT MAKES A NUTRITIOUS DIET?

Without wanting to go into the detail of all the nutrients we need to get from our diet, and where you can find them, I'd like to make a few simple suggestions, which if you follow them, will maximise the amount of nutrition you get on a daily basis.

Aim to eat foods which are as whole and unprocessed as possible

Obviously preparing meals from scratch is the best option, however it can be a bit of a leap to make when you are short of time, and you don't come home from work before 7pm, feeling ravenous. So let's say it's something to aim for, but there are gradual steps you can take towards this.

Simple recipes and batch cooking

Of course, no-one with a busy work schedule is going to spend hours preparing food. It just wouldn't be practical. There are ways of making this process as efficient as possible. The recipe section later on gives you a selection of recipes which can be done in under 15 minutes, as well as some which you can 'batch-cook'. This means that when you have some spare time, over the weekend perhaps, you can prepare a large quantity (which won't necessarily take that long) and then put portions away to eat during the week.

More raw

The other consideration regarding processing is how you prepare food at home. Ideally you should eat a good proportion of your plant foods raw or very lightly cooked. Heat destroys a lot of nutrients and vital enzymes in your vegetables, so start questioning whether you need to cook everything – perhaps you'd enjoy those sugar snap peas just as much if not more, if they were raw, and the same goes with peppers, cauliflower, etc... Think about having raw grated beetroot or even courgettes, and of course getting into the habit of having a raw side salad is always a good thing.

Re-evaluating your priorities

Often part of the process is changing your mindset around how important what you eat is to you. If nutrition is very low down the priority list, then even 10 minutes spent preparing food might seem like a waste of time. The more value you put on your health and wellbeing, and notice the impact food has on how you feel, the more important it will feel to allocate some time to preparing food as part of your daily routine.

Are you worth it?
One of my clients, Tony Kensington, who owns an accountancy practice, achieved a complete transformation, just as a result of attending a talk I gave in 2013. Thanks to his dedication to following the advice I gave, and with very little outside support, he lost 32lbs and his metabolic age (as measured on the Tanita scales) fell from 48 to 34. When I asked him to share his advice so that others could be inspired by his story, his answer didn't disappoint.

He said: "You can't underestimate the investment that does need to be made. And first of all decide whether you're worth it. Have your L'Oreal moment as I call it! 'Am I worth doing it? Because if you're not then don't do it. You need to sort yourself out, and your mind first. I feel much better off as a result of investing in my health and wellbeing."

So, what is your mind saying to you? Have you had your L'Oreal moment yet? Or are you just looking for excuses because your wellbeing hasn't really made it to the top of your priority list?

VARIETY IS THE SPICE OF LIFE

It's very easy to slip into a daily routine of always eating the same things, because it takes less 'thinking energy', particularly when it comes to shopping. It's so much easier to just go round the aisles in the supermarket picking up the same items week in, week out. Everyone has a repertoire of dishes they go through each week and that's perfectly ok. I'm not saying you should complicate things too much.

Perhaps you could make the same dishes, but vary the vegetables you use in them according to what's seasonal? I always used to use exactly the same vegetables in my Thai green curry, no matter what time of year. And then I subscribed to an organic veg box, which meant I had to start using all kinds of different vegetables: cauliflower, Jerusalem artichokes, kale... whatever I have in the fridge goes in the pot. And nowadays I really enjoy the variety, and look forward to the flavours of foods which are in season (and haven't flown thousands of miles in refrigeration chambers).

As a basic guideline for plant foods, it's always a good idea to aim for a wide range of colours, as each type of pigment reflects specific plant nutrients which your body will thank you for.

KNOW THE MYTHS

Many people's diets are nutritionally deficient, because the information they've heard wasn't accurate. This is because there are some very common myths which have become widespread. Let's examine a few.

MYTH ALERT! You can easily over-do the protein and damage your kidneys

People often view protein with suspicion – too much can damage your kidneys, can't it?

Actually, there's no evidence anywhere in the scientific literature that healthy kidneys are damaged by protein, even in quantities 2–3 times above the Recommended Dietary Allowance (RDA)[7].

The consensus generally around protein requirements is that you need around 1g of pure protein per Kg body weight, and more if you exercise. So if you weigh 70Kg, then you should be consuming at least 70g of pure protein. Check the protein traffic light tables in the resources section of my website to see what this amounts to in terms of specific foods (http://www.superwellness.co.uk/eat-well-at-work/resources). Just as a guideline, an egg contains around 5g of pure protein, a medium fillet of chicken around 25g and a handful of cooked lentils gives you around 8g.

Protein is mostly deficient in people's diets – carbohydrates are much cheaper, so most convenience foods major on them. The average sandwich has a lot of bread for a small amount of protein filling.

MYTH ALERT! Fat is bad for you

There was a time when it was believed that fats shouldn't make up more than 10% of our diet. Science has come a long way since then, and we now know that this amount is woefully inadequate. Fat is a vital ingredient for our body, providing the raw material for many of our hormones, every single one of our cell membranes and most of the protective covering of our nerves. Our brain is 60% fats... so a 'low fat' diet is the opposite of healthy.

This is why modern food labelling can be very misleading, with the 'traffic light' system highlighting foods with a high fat content as 'red' (which would seem to say 'unhealthy'). For this reason, many still believe that nuts are bad, because they are 'full of fat'. The same goes with coconut milk and avocados. What a joy when my clients realise they can bring those foods back into their diets.

Even saturated fat is not as bad as it was once believed. In fact butter has recently been officially rehabilitated[1]. It is officially healthier for you than the 'low fat spreads' which contain additives and often trans-fats too. Recent studies have shown that there is no connection between fat in the diet and cardiovascular disease. Hard to believe when the low fat mantra has been playing on a loop for so long! And yet, the research is there to prove it.

VEGETARIAN AND VEGAN DIETS

It's estimated that 1 in 8 adults in the UK are vegetarian or vegan, rising to 1 in 5 among 16 to 24 year olds (according to a report by Mintel published in October 2014). If you don't eat meat, fish, or any other animal products, then that is a healthy move in some respects, but only if you make sure you are getting the nutrients you need from other sources.

So what are the main nutrients to look out for if you are a veggie?

Protein

Getting the right amounts of protein can be challenging for vegetarians. With the right kind of planning though, the challenge can be easily overcome. Just a few words of advice here if your diet is free of meat and fish, or any animal products at all.

Protein is made up of amino-acids, some of which are essential, in other words, if your diet doesn't provide them, your body can't make them. Bearing in mind that these amino acids are the materials your body uses to make up specific brain chemicals, hormones, or nerve tissue (and the list goes on), it's pretty clear that if you don't pay attention to them, problems will emerge. The connection between these problems and lack of protein won't be obvious necessarily – perhaps you might begin to feel a bit low, or find that no matter how much you work out in the gym, you're still losing muscle.

Vegetarian protein foods are often incomplete because they only contain some of the essential amino acids. This is why it's important to get a wide variety in your diet – for example: lentils and pulses, nuts and seeds and tofu.

It used to be said that vegetarians had to get a combination of these eight essential amino acids in the same meal, combining various pulses to do this. We now know that it doesn't have to be that complicated. But you do need to get the balance right overall, making sure that each meal includes some plant protein and that they vary throughout the week.

If you are vegetarian as opposed to vegan, then good quality eggs (organic free range) are a perfect source of all of the amino acids you need. Dairy foods in moderation (I say 'in moderation' because of the high levels of hormones they contain, and frequent intolerances to lactose or casein) can be a good source. For the sake of practicality, when I work with vegetarian clients who really struggle to plan for adequate protein, I often recommend the use of protein powders. They are available from a variety of sources (like whey, hemp, pea or rice) and can be made into healthy breakfast shakes (see the recipe section and check my website for my product recommendations http://www.superwellness.co.uk/eat-well-at-work/recommended-suppliers/). Protein powder can even be added to porridge, soup or cakes.

So let's turn to good plant sources of protein, and the first thing to mention is that lentils and pulses are an undervalued bonanza. They are inexpensive, and yet highly nutritious, tasty and varied. They provide a combination of protein and fibre-rich, slow-burning carbohydrates, not to mention all the vitamins and minerals.

Their variety is truly astonishing, spanning a vast range of flavours and textures (just in the lentils department, red are good for dhal, green and brown for everyday use, 'puy' are lovely and nutty, and my favourite: beluga lentils – jet black with an incredibly rich flavour and texture). And the beans! Chickpeas, Cannellini beans, Butter beans, Pinto beans, Black beans, Kidney beans have starring roles in so many tasty international dishes from Moroccan to Mexican, and are delicious in stews, soups, salads and dips. So versatile!

Preparing them doesn't have to be time-consuming. Both beans and lentils can be bought in cans, rinsed and drained for a healthy convenience food.

Quinoa: a real superfood. Quinoa is not only a complete protein (containing all of the essential amino acids), it is also an incredibly rich source of vitamins and minerals. It takes 10 minutes to prepare. I usually simmer in some water with an added teaspoon of turmeric and Swiss vegetable bouillon powder.

It can be eaten hot, as an alternative to rice, or cold, in a salad, and makes a great 'on the run' snack with veggies or chickpeas mixed into it.

You can even freeze portions of it for quick use when you get home from work.

Iron

This mineral is vital for us to make enough haemoglobin for the red cells in our blood to be able to transport vital oxygen to all of the tissues around the body.

Iron is also necessary to support proper metabolism for muscles and other active organs. When your cells burn dietary calories to create energy, this process requires iron. So when iron stores get low, your cells struggle to produce energy and you begin to feel fatigued. The result of low iron stores is anaemia.

Among plant foods, leafy green vegetables, lentils and some herbs and spices are among our best sources. Spinach, chard and asparagus top the list along with pepper, cumin, turmeric and thyme.

B12

More insidious than iron deficiency anaemia, B12 deficiency is rather common and very dangerous.

Some of the tell tale signs and symptoms can often be interpreted as the result of other issues and they include nervousness, numb feet, depression, fatigue, palpitations, sore tongue and dandruff.

B12 is vital in the maturation of red blood cells. Without B12, we can't synthesise the DNA needed to provide the information for this to happen. The cells become oversized and poorly shaped, and begin to function ineffectively, a condition called pernicious anaemia.

Lack of B12 is also a threat to healthy nerves, as it is needed for us to maintain a coating which protects the nerves , called the myelin sheath.

B12 is mainly supplied from animal sources, but is also available in some fermented foods. So it's very important for vegetarians to include some cultured and fermented bean products like tofu, tempeh, miso, tamari and shoyu in their diet. Brewer's and nutritional yeast can also be good sources.

Personally I would usually recommend vegetarians request regular blood checks from their doctor and supplement if needed, and if levels are really low, then B12 injections may be required.

Iodine

Iodine, a trace mineral, is required by the body for the thyroid to synthesize thyroid hormones, responsible for regulating metabolism in every cell of the body. An iodine deficiency can have a devastating impact on your health and well-being, and lead to symptoms such as fatigue, weight gain, weakness and depression. Severe iodine deficiency during pregnancy or infancy can cause developmental problems, stunted growth and deafness.

For vegetarians, sea vegetables are an excellent source. You can now easily buy various exciting types of sea vegetables in the supermarkets. They come in dry form and all you have to do is leave them to soak in hot water for a few minutes. Yogurt, mozzarella cheese, eggs, and strawberries are also good sources.

2 Principle # 2: Balancing the metabolism with a low glycaemic load diet

The term metabolism essentially means the process which what we eat undergoes in our body – how the food you eat gets turned into energy, how it becomes new cells, and how it performs other essential functions which allow life to continue and hopefully thrive.

A key part of this is how our cells use glucose as a source of energy. Nowadays, with diets high in sugar and carbohydrates, our ability to regulate this process can fall out of balance. Many people experience a 'blood sugar rollercoaster' throughout the day, where they get a short burst of energy from carbohydrate foods (which break down into glucose in the blood), then go through a 'crash' an hour later, making them crave more bread or pasta, causing this 'up and down' pattern to continue indefinitely.

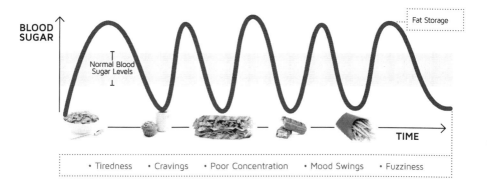

Highs and lows in blood sugar play havoc with our metabolism and end up causing us to store fat, put on weight and suffer from low energy and cravings (as well as poor concentration, irregular moods, and the list goes on...)

MYTH ALERT! 'Normal' blood glucose means all is well

You may get your fasting glucose checked by your doctor and find that you are in the 'normal' range, Does this mean you are not affected by these highs and lows?

Far from it. Because for a long time, your body can compensate for these ups and downs thanks to a hormone called insulin, keeping your blood sugars normal, but wreaking havoc behind the scenes. Insulin's role is to introduce glucose into the cells, where it can be turned into energy. The more frequently your pancreas releases insulin, the more resistant your cells will become to it, leading to a widespread problem called insulin resistance. We'll come to that in a moment.

The most up to date unit of measurement of a food's impact on blood sugars is called Glycaemic Load (GL). A food's GL reflects how much sugar it will release in the blood, and how fast. A high GL food will produce a sugar spike, followed by the familiar sugar 'low'.

The food group to pay attention to in terms of GL impact is carbohydrates (which include a wide range of foods from the very starchy, low fibre – white pasta, white bread, white rice – to the very low starch, high fibre – green leafy vegetables, tomatoes and peppers for example .

Very starchy	low starch
Low fibre	high fibre
White pasta,	Spinach
White bread,	Tomatoes
White rice	Peppers

The foods to the left of this line have the highest GL value and the ones to the right of the line have the lowest. Essentially, the more refined a food is, the closer it is to glucose, and the faster it will drive up blood glucose levels too.

To get familiar with the practical side of Glycaemic Load, take a look at Chapter 3, Habit 3: Being carb-savvy.

WHAT HAPPENS WHEN YOU EAT HIGH GL FOODS?
When blood sugars are high, after high GL foods, the body does everything it can to drive the levels down again, as too much sugar in the blood is bad news (sugar is very corrosive and damages blood vessels).

How does the body reduce blood sugar levels?

The pancreas releases the hormone insulin, which is necessary to introduce glucose into the cells, where it can be turned into energy

However the cells can only process a limited amount of glucose at a time. If there is still too much glucose left in the bloodstream, insulin then carries it to the glycogen stores (an emergency store of glucose) in the muscles and liver.

Once the glycogen stores become full, any remaining excess glucose gets stored in the fat cells.

When we eat these foods in excess day in, day out, this stimulates repeated sharp spikes in insulin being released. This in turn can eventually result in the insulin 'overshooting' the mark, and driving blood sugar levels down very abruptly. This is what causes frequent energy 'crashes', which we experience as ongoing tiredness (and reliance upon caffeine!), cravings, mood swings, lack of concentration and fuzziness.

Eventually, as I mentioned earlier, the insulin receptors on the cell become resistant to insulin because they are overwhelmed. This means insulin is no longer doing its job of introducing glucose into the cell.

The cell begins to lack glucose to produce energy, which is why someone with insulin resistance will often feel fatigued.

Meanwhile, the levels of insulin in the body start to increase (in the UK, fasting blood glucose is often measured, but fasting insulin rarely is!) and the problem with this, which we touched on earlier, is that insulin sets the metabolism to 'fat storing' mode. Not only does it facilitate fat storage, it also inhibits fat burning (even if you hit the gym) and promotes weight gain, especially around the abdomen.

As insulin's mechanisms become more and more out of balance, it in turn struggles to do its job of keeping glucose levels in check, which eventually, in some people, can lead to type 2 diabetes. Way before diabetes becomes full blown, insulin resistance can wreak havoc in the body, causing low energy, weight gain and disrupting other hormones.

HOW DO YOU BALANCE BLOOD SUGARS?

If you struggle with cravings, feeling that your eating is 'out of control' (perhaps with the guilt which goes along with this), and get energy lows a couple of hours after meals, then this is a good place to begin for you.

This is usually where I start with my clients, and in doing so, the changes we make to their diet start to benefit the other two core principles too (they'll start to feed their body more nutrients, as well as being kinder to their digestive system).

This phase usually takes around a month when I'm working with a client, and by then, they are starting to feel a big difference already. The important thing to remember is that you can't change all your habits overnight, and in no context is this truer than this one: blood sugar balancing.

Mainly because the biggest part of this step is reducing your sugar intake. Make no mistake: sugar is incredibly addictive, and willpower alone doesn't stand much of a chance of overcoming this physiological property. Professor Robert Lustig in the United States is one of the scientists who has raised the alarm about the dangers of sugar. Thanks to his book 'Sugar: the bitter truth' and numerous public appearances, the mainstream press has picked up on the public health disaster spelt by our modern sugar-laden diets. The mantra that 'sugar in itself is quite innocent, it's individuals' lack of restraint which is the problem' is beginning to sound resonantly hollow in the face of all the mounting scientific evidence against it.

MYTH ALERT! A good diet is about 'everything in moderation' and nothing is bad as long as it's part of a 'balanced diet'

These statements seem at worst bland and harmless, and yet they set the stage for the nutritional aberrations which gradually erode millions of people's health on a yearly basis.

Apart from the fact that both are incredibly vague and unscientific, they also conveniently take the spotlight away from the food itself (and those who produce it) and squarely shine it on the consumer, who's made responsible for mismanaging his/her own choices. So on the one hand, you have these sensible sounding but vague guidelines, and on the other hand, the extremely powerful and to many, irresistible, multi billion pound food advertising machinery. One can't underestimate the impact of advertising constantly sending your subconscious mind the message that such and such a sugar and caffeine laden drink will give you super powers. Or equating an additive laden snack with looking cool when you entertain your friends.

You've got to ask yourself: what chance does a person stand of applying moderation to foods which trigger a spiral of addiction? How helpful is a diet which balances 'healthy' foods with others which throw our metabolism out of whack? And another question: is one packet of crisps a day 'in moderation'? Or is 365 packets of crisps a year an unacceptable burden for the body to bear? When you have a certain food type every day, even if it's just a small part of your daily intake, it amounts to a lot over the years.

So let me share with you the balance of food types which work for my clients, enabling sugar cravings to fade away, and a feeling of control to be restored.

AVOIDING BLOOD SUGAR SPIKES

One of the first steps is to start decreasing the foods which cause these spikes: sugar, whether it's added to foods or not and the most refined types of carbohydrates. Fruit sugars and so called 'natural sugars' are just as harmful as the sugar you add to a cup of tea. In fact fructose, long believed to be healthier than glucose, gets converted straight into fat in the liver area, but that's another story. When you first begin to reduce sugar, you may well experience some withdrawal symptoms, and initially your cravings are likely to get worse. If your cells have developed a certain level of insulin resistance, then you'll be getting a lot less energy from your sugar intake, driving you to feel that you need more and more... reducing it goes against the grain!

HANDLING THE 'LOWS'

There is a secret however to making this process a whole lot easier – and that's protein. The vast majority of people have a diet which is deficient in good quality protein, and yet it is the building block for every tissue in our body, and many of the chemicals which keep us functioning.

No wonder that when you start having adequate amounts of it, suddenly cravings just seem to disappear. You begin to feel satisfied and nourished, rather than being constantly obsessed with what to eat next. So the secret is this: as you begin to 'de-sugar-ize', just make sure you include good amounts of protein as part of every single meal you have. It could mean having eggs in the morning, snacking on some nuts or seeds, switching your lunchtime sandwich which has only a sliver of cheese in it to a chicken salad, containing at least the equivalent of a medium sized fillet.

The other technique for making this transition period as easy as possible for you is to eat the right things often. This is where snacks come in, as they avoid the 'low' you might experience 2 or 3 hours after breakfast or lunch. As your blood sugars get more and more even, you might find you don't even need these snacks any more, and your eating feels much more under control.

Principle #3: digestion and detoxification

3

Nutrition is not just about the food we eat, it also has to do with how our body *interacts* with the food. Our ability to draw nourishment from it and to get rid of the waste created in the process – to 'detoxify'. The health of our digestive function is crucial for this to happen optimally.

More and more important discoveries are being made about the role played by our gut bacteria, also known as our 'microbiome'. We have ten times more bacteria in our gut than cells in our body, and together, they act like a huge processing plant for everything that goes into your body. Like an array of sophisticated machines designed for specific functions: breaking down raw materials coming in to allow the nutrients into your blood stream, turning the raw materials into vitamins, like B and K, neutralising threatening microorganisms, and even deciding how many calories are extracted from the food, thereby contributing to someone's tendency to become obese[8].

It turns out your gut doesn't just house this giant processing plant, it also serves as your body's main army base, with 70% of your immune cells situated in the gastro-intestinal tract, and general government headquarters, with overall half of your neurotransmitters (usually referred to as 'brain chemicals') residing there. In fact, our gut has been dubbed the 'second brain' because so much of the chemistry which affects how we feel takes place here. 90% of the body's serotonin (the 'happy' hormone) resides in the gut.

It's not surprising that our gut is often referred to as 'the seat of health' and this is why optimising digestive function is a key part of any effective nutrition programme.

So what are the practical steps you can take?

1. EAT CONSCIOUSLY
Today's busy lifestyle makes stress all pervasive, because we are constantly bombarded with information, and our lives are much more complex than they used to be. Instead of short, sharp bursts of stress, we have to deal with ongoing, chronic stress and over time, this can have devastating effects on the digestive system.

If you try to eat while stressed (or in 'flight or fight' mode), your nervous system will be directing all of your body's resources towards functions it considers necessary for dealing with an emergency situation (like facing a sabre tooth tiger!) It will be diverting resources away from digestion, because it is not immediately necessary for survival.

Although most people think of stress as *emotional* stress caused by pressure at work, or disagreements with other people, in fact there are many more sources of stress. Simply looking at the screen of an electronic device is a stressor for the brain. The flickering light and huge amounts of data overwhelm our normal processing capacity, no matter what we are looking at. Imagine then, how much worse the stress gets when you are watching a disturbing movie, or simply a news report, while eating your dinner!

And it's not just the switch into 'fight or flight' mode which is undesirable, it's also the fact that our attention is being diverted away from what we are doing, leading to unconscious eating. This means we don't savour the food as much, forget to chew sufficiently, and often end up eating much more than we really need to. It's amazing how many people have a TV in the areas of their homes where they eat their meals, and how many eat their lunch at their desk whilst staring at a computer screen. Changing these habits will have hugely beneficial results.

When your body is in 'rest and digest' mode, your nervous system will be geared to 'pressing all the right buttons' for the complex digestive processes to take place. This means you'll benefit from optimal digestion and absorption of the nutrients from your food.

How to switch into 'rest and digest'?

- Avoid looking at a screen while you're eating
- Move away from your desk and sit somewhere where you can be relaxed
- Chew each mouthful well to make sure your food is coated with digestive enzymes, easing the process of breaking down the food further downstream.

2. DITCH THE IRRITANTS

Our intestinal wall is a thin, but very precious barrier between the outside world (food and drink, medicines, chemicals, etc...) and our internal system, especially the immune system. It allows through nutrients which are then carried to the cells via the bloodstream, and it is designed to protect us from toxins and bacteria which would be very harmful were they to make it into our bloodstream.

Sometimes however this thin barrier can become compromised, jeopardising this protective role, and resulting in increased activity from the immune system. This is a well studied phenomenon called 'leaky gut', or 'intestinal membrane permeability'. It means that widened gaps in the digestive membrane allow food particles, chemicals or gut bacteria to travel through[9]. The immune system mobilizes to attack these 'invaders' and marks offending food molecules as 'undesirable'. The end result can be food intolerances appearing which hadn't been there before. You might have experienced this or know someone who has: suddenly eating bread starts to make you feel bloated, or a rash appears when you eat cucumbers!

So what are these irritants which compromise our intestinal lining in the first place?

- Strong chemicals from alcohol, caffeine or cigarette smoke

- Chemical additives and preservatives from foods, as well as from personal care and cosmetic products, which all penetrate the blood stream through the skin

- Excessive sugar, an irritant in its own right and the favourite food for yeasts which reside in the gut. They thrive on it, take over the place and cause even more damage

- Food which hasn't been well chewed, leading to fermentation or putrefaction in the intestines (nice thought!)

- Antibiotics, although sometimes necessary, can unintentionally destroy protective bacteria, allowing harmful bacteria to thrive

- Foods which your immune army has earmarked, so that every time you eat them, the artillery gets wheeled out, and your gut turns into a battle field

- Finally, stress. Believe me, its effects are very tangible, and even your gut lining pays the price, as protein gets 'stolen' from it in order to be used elsewhere, where it's perceived to be needed more urgently. Imagine this happening over the course of weeks, months and years of the kind of simmering stress which most people experience day in day out nowadays – our internal protection is wearing thin!

MORE ABOUT FOOD SENSITIVITIES

It's possible to be allergic or intolerant to certain foods. An allergy is an immediate reaction, which can have varying degrees, from swelling or itchiness to actually endangering your life. Food intolerances are much more difficult to detect as the immune system can take up to 72 hours to react to the offending food. This means that the symptoms are not obviously related to the food, and people can continue damaging their health for months or even years without knowing what they are doing wrong, all the while suffering 'unexplained symptoms'.

In food intolerance, the immune system produces a type of antibody called IgG (Immunoglobulin G) in reaction to a food which it sees as an undesirable 'invader'. This can develop as a result of eating the same foods too often (which is a good reason for varying your diet as much as you can), and of the phenomenon mentioned above - leaky gut - where microscopic particles of food pass through widened gaps in the intestinal membrane.

The most common culprits when it comes to food intolerances are gluten (a protein found in wheat), lactose and casein (both found in cow's milk). Other suspects include eggs, seafood, nuts and yeast, however people also react very individually to specific foods. Sometimes this can happen because they eat a specific food too often, over-exposing their immune system to it in the process. I would recommend keeping a food diary for a couple of weeks, noting down every single food and drink which enters your mouth and tracking symptoms such as bloating, gas, changes in bowel movement, headaches or energy ups and downs.

It's worth speaking to a qualified Nutritional Therapist about doing an elimination diet, in which you avoid suspected food types for at least a month, and then reintroduce them one by one to see how this affects symptoms. There are also blood tests which can be done to identify food intolerances (showing IgG antibodies to relevant foods), and it's important to use a reputable laboratory with good quality control to do so (again a professional Nutritional Therapist can point you in the right direction and help you with nutritious substitutes once you've found the culprits.)

By being gentle to your intestinal membrane, and avoiding foods your immune system reacts to, you'll reduce inflammation and vastly increase the percentage of nutrients you get from your food. A well nourished body is much less hungry for food, and functions optimally to give you energy, burn fat and keep you in your peak state of wellness.

3. KEEP IT MOVING

As well as absorbing nutrients, our digestive system has a massive responsibility for keeping our body clean and free of toxins. A sluggish digestive flow means that toxins from food waste remain longer in the bowel instead of moving through to be evacuated. Some of these toxins are reabsorbed through the gut wall and re-circulated in the blood stream. This in turn puts pressure on the liver, whose role it is to filter toxins out of the blood. If our ability to clear this waste gets overwhelmed, this burden of toxicity impacts our whole body, even at the minutest cellular level.

Imagine a city whose waste disposal staff have gone on strike. Mountains of bin liners piling up at every street corner... eventually they begin to fester, leak and smell. If this continued for too long, it would cause disease and bring the city to a standstill.

So how do you keep your digestive system flowing?

- Drink at least 1.5 litres of fresh water a day
- Make sure you get lots of good fibre
- Top up your pre- and probiotics

In light of all the irritants we are exposed to, it's easy to understand why the complex balance of bacteria can become compromised – especially if you have undergone several courses of antibiotics in your lifetime. So how do you re-establish a healthy balance?

Prebiotics: feed the good bacteria

There are certain foods which are nectar for our beneficial bacteria and will help them to thrive. They include: leeks, onions, garlic, Jerusalem artichokes and oats.

Probiotics: top up the levels

There has been a lot of marketing in recent years for various products said to provide 'good bacteria'. I would strongly advise caution and discrimination in choosing products which are truly effective. I would completely avoid any sweetened little yoghurt pots claiming to have these effects as the sugar or sweeteners they contain tend to eliminate any positive effects they might have. If you wish to supplement with a good quality probiotic, then tread carefully, and ask for advice in a health food shop with well trained staff, or even better, consult with a qualified Nutritional Therapist. They will be able to recommend specific strains to match your personal needs. The optimum approach, if you take your gut health really seriously, is to carry out a comprehensive stool analysis with a reputable laboratory, which a Nutritional Therapist can analyse for you before making the most relevant recommendations. An investment in the short term, but a saving in the long term, because you are targeting your specific needs rather than wasting money and time taking supplements which are not 'quite' appropriate for you.

So now that we've taken in the three key principles for you to get started, how do you begin planning for 'project health'?

Chapter 2: Planning for 'project health'

> **Give me six hours to chop down a tree, and I will spend the first four hours sharpening the axe."**
> Abraham Lincoln

If you've tried to change habits before, you'll no doubt know that it can be a baffling process. Some habits seem to fall into place effortlessly, whilst others need endless repeated attempts, with no sign of success. Why is this?

If you're like most people, you might feel like blaming yourself, and your 'lack of willpower'. Why can't your rational self get the better of cravings and that urge to fall back into old patterns?

Well the good news is, you no longer have to beat yourself up, because what you interpret as weakness is in fact just normal human behaviour. It's how we are all programmed to function, and by understanding the process scientifically, you can also have more influence over it.

In the past 50 years, the science of behavioural change has made major breakthroughs. The work which most got my attention is the large scale research carried out by James Prochaska, John Norcross and Carlo Diclemente since the late 1970s. These scientists wanted to understand why some people managed to give up smoking overnight, whilst others made failed attempt after failed attempt. They compiled a model from their findings, gathered across dozens of studies involving thousands of subjects. In one Eureka moment, tables of seemingly baffling and random data suddenly clicked into place.

CHANGING FOR GOOD
What Prochaska and his colleagues had discovered was that essentially change is a process, not a single event. And this process has six stages. There are no shortcuts, although it is possible to work on each stage and speed it up.

When I read about this, it made total sense. If you're in denial about needing to make a change (the first stage), you're just not going to. It doesn't matter how many other people think you should! You'll need some kind of prompt to change your mind, maybe a colleague strides up the stairs past you and suddenly in that moment, you realise how fed up you are of feeling tired and devoid of energy. You might identify with some of these common prompts my clients mention when I ask them what it was that finally nudged them towards taking action:

- Brain fuzz: realising that for quite some time, you've been unable to follow a train of thought clearly, the impression of going round in circles in your head, trying to focus desperately. And before you know it, two hours have gone by, and that report is still decidedly unfinished.

- Feeling out of control. I worked with a client, Chris, who described this predicament: "I was in a real mess. I felt awful, I was constantly feeling hungry, and it didn't seem to matter how much I ate, I never felt like I was satisfied. I was starting to feel completely out of control". And it wasn't as if Chris was not a disciplined person: several triathlons under his belt, including ironman contests, he was the last person you'd accuse of being 'lazy' or 'undisciplined'.

- Noticing that you rely far too much on stimulants to function: do you need three coffees to get going in the morning? Do you regularly stop 'en route' to a destination to pick up a Red Bull or Coke? Then you're being artificially propped up by adrenaline, a stress hormone only meant for extreme circumstances, not everyday living, and at some stage it's likely to fail, leaving you burnt out.

- If 'sugarholics anonymous' existed, you would be thinking of joining it. That mid-morning muffin or afternoon chocolate bar is no longer a choice, it's a matter of life or death! Some of my clients even recall waking up during the night desperate for a sugar fix.

- A 'creaking' body: aches and pains which are not exactly life threatening and don't quite warrant a medical diagnosis. You do your best not to notice them and just put them down to 'getting old', but surely this isn't as good as it gets?

- Increasingly disturbing digestive upsets, from wind and bloating to cramps, and even close calls, or at the other end of the spectrum, the inability to go to the toilet for days.

These are the most common reasons people visit me in my nutrition clinic and usually they've been experiencing them for quite some time. The fear of having to let go of habits formed over years can be a huge obstacle – you may have experienced the feeling yourself? You know you ought to do something but in your mind the benefits of doing so don't quite outweigh the sacrifices that would involve – yet. Again, all part of the process of contemplating change.

It can take a desperate situation to finally overcome it (when for example the threat of getting caught out without a toilet becomes an intolerable source of stress). At the other end of the scale, excitement and inspiration can also be huge catalysts for change.

CULTIVATING INSPIRATION
Inspiration is a powerful feeling that can propel you forward, making change easy and rewarding. In my experience, it's something which can be cultivated. You've probably had the experience of reading a book, or an article, or watching something which moved you to start doing something differently? Look at the power of Olympic athletes to inspire millions to go out on their bikes after the London Olympics, or join running clubs. And when Jamie Oliver's documentary about intensively farmed chickens was aired, many were moved to change this particular shopping habit. What could you watch, or read, which will fill you with transformative energy and determination?

In the past few years there have been many books, films and documentaries which have inspired me to make changes, drastically speeding up the process of contemplating change. Visit my website http://www.superwellness.co.uk/eat-well-at-work/resources/ to find a list of links and resources which have worked for me and for my clients.

DOING YOUR RESEARCH

Once you've decided to ring the changes, your next step will be to research your options. This is how you build the confidence you need to know you're on the right track.

This is where all the conflicting information about nutrition can really take its toll. You've no doubt met people who are constantly trying new diets? Or perhaps you've been there yourself? It can end up feeling as though there is no way out. None of the diets bring long term results but you're afraid to give up on dieting for fear of being even worse off. This is why it's so important to cut through all of this confusion and get some clear reference points which you can trust.

In my view, there is only one trustworthy source: up to date scientific research. Research carried out by independent sources (trying to avoid those who are defending specific interests, or supporting particular industries).

I HAVE A HEALTHY DIET, AND YET...

This is how the conversation begins with many of my new clients – most people believe they already have a healthy diet, and yet they still battle with diet related problems – why would this be?

Simply because our perception of what a 'healthy diet' means is seriously flawed.

It's hard to deny the commercial and political interests that influence messages about 'healthy eating'. The food industry is driven by market forces and is hugely powerful and influential. Food advertising is everywhere. Highly trained PR teams help shape media perceptions, and lobbyists influence government guidelines.

No-one can blame food companies for wanting to make profits.

Hence the packaging boldly claiming contents to be 'heart healthy', 'one of your five a day', or 'wholesome'. Never mind the unhealthy levels of sugar or chemicals also included in the package.

This is why it's so important never to place your health interests unquestioningly into someone else's hands. Make sure you always look at the motives behind any information you read and trust your instincts and your own experience.

The advice I'm sharing in this book draws on scientific sources, and it also reflects my own experience of what has worked for my clients, and for myself. If it makes sense to you, if it feels right, then I invite you to put it into practice for at least 6 weeks. When you begin to experience the results, feel differently and integrate the new habits, you'll be paving the way to long term lifestyle change.

TIME (LACK OF!)

Much as 'work-life balance' is a popular (and necessary) topic, unfortunately a lot of people are a long way from achieving it. I sincerely hope that you are one of the few who have mastered the art of making your work fit in with your chosen lifestyle, as written about so inspiringly by Tim Ferriss in 'The 4 Hour Work Week.'

If you're not there yet however, then you probably are faced with exactly the same challenge as most of my professional clients: a perceived lack of time. The feeling of being trapped in a busy schedule, a sense of being carried away by a strong current from the moment you wake up to the moment you fall asleep.

You leave home early in the morning, you've barely got time to grab a sandwich at your desk at lunchtime, if you're not actually in your car, racing to a client meeting. You're away on business trips, or entertaining clients, leaving you with restricted food choices. Taking 10 minutes out to prepare dinner seems like a tall order when you're already behind with your proposal, and will probably be burning the midnight oil anyway.

THE COMMITMENT TO STICK WITH IT

The thing is, whatever work you do, there are certain constraints which are not going to disappear overnight. Quite simply, you've got to do the best you can with what you've got, and above all, never beat yourself up when things turn out less than perfectly.

The most important ingredient which will see you through is your commitment. Not the commitment to be perfect, but the commitment to stick with it even though things are less than perfect.

If you seriously intend to change long standing habits, then you need to know about this and be prepared for it. Having got this out of the way, there's a number of things you can do to work around a busy work schedule.

PLANNING

Planning is essential. Being prepared means that when you are on auto-pilot in the morning, you won't have to think twice about breakfast. When you are rushing from one work meeting to the next, you won't have to improvise your snacks (leaving yourself wide open to other temptations!). And when you return home in the evening, you won't have to summon your last resources of energy to devise a menu, and get cooking. Because let's face it, without preparation and planning, the easiest option is always likely to prevail. And the takeaway pizza menu will seem extremely attractive all of a sudden.

SO WHAT'S THE BEST WAY TO PLAN?

Have a look at your schedule for the coming weeks and try to spot any challenging times ahead. If you have a week-long business trip planned, be prepared to relax about slower progress during that week. When would be a good time to start? When can you fit in a good food shopping trip (or online shopping session) in preparation for it?

Just as you would make a plan for your business activities during the week, you can also make a plan for food and exercise. Imagine if you approached every business task at the last minute – called people up to have meetings the same day, or prepared for a client pitch 5 minutes before seeing them... you would probably not be in business (or in the job) for very long, because you would waste so much time and energy through lack of preparation. Why should your personal health and wellbeing suffer from such ineffective strategies? You can use the diary to schedule exercise, and even well-needed relaxation, like going for a walk. A quick 10 minutes to plan your meals throughout the week makes it easier to organise your weekly supplies (placing an order online only takes a few minutes and saves so much hassle). Your eating doesn't have to be chaotic because of a busy schedule, it can just become a part of the schedule

One of my clients, Stephanie, works for a talent agency. Sometimes, she's out three evenings a week networking at functions or visiting shows. An exciting whirlwind of activity, but very disruptive of a healthy routine! In the past she had almost given up on trying to be healthy. After all, she couldn't get out of these social commitments. Where could she go from there?

One of the first things we did was to put the situation into perspective. 3 evenings a week seems like a lot, but actually, that's just 3 meals out of 21 in a week. If she can be 'good' the rest of the time, then we are still well within the 80/20 rule.

Then taking it a little further, we explored ways we might even be able to make these 'showbiz' evenings as healthy as possible. Stephanie began having substantial and healthy snacks before leaving for these functions. This meant she didn't need to pick on unhealthy nibbles or be tempted by poor choices later. We came up with a couple of ideas for very quick and easy refuelling once she got home, even though it might be late at night. We also worked on her mindset, so that, should things go wrong, her first thought the next day was: 'Oh well, that's behind me now. I'll just get back to it today and keep going.' This approach helped her to feel in control and rise above every day challenges so that she could stay focused on her long term goals.

So here are some strategies for you to consider, which should help you work with and around, rather than against your work schedule:

- Plan and prepare your meals – just as you do your work activities

- Apply the 80/20 rule – make the healthiest possible choices when you are in control

- Damage limitation – things can't always be perfect, but can you fuel up on a healthy snack before or after so that you are in control when temptation is around?

Now let's look at ways you can stay strong mentally to pull off 'project health' in the long term.

GET THE SUCCESS MINDSET

Identify your 'bright spots': what are your biggest strengths which will support you in this process? List them. Perhaps you are well organised, or a good project manager at work? Then approach this like a project. What needs to happen? By when? And who can help you make it happen?

Do you need support? A nutrition coach? A personal trainer? An accountability coach?

Identify your personal challenges and how you could overcome them. It could be that for you, emotional eating is your biggest downfall, or peer pressure, or the fact you don't enjoy preparing food. In what ways could you minimise their impact and stop them becoming major showstoppers?

RECRUIT YOUR PROJECT TEAM

Who in your social or work circle is most likely to support you towards achieving your goals?

It might be someone with similar goals, with whom you could buddy up and perhaps even share meals at work. As well as the moral support, this can give you a sense of accountability which is very powerful.

Most people can't bear the thought of letting others down, or being seen to fail. Having people know what you're aiming for is the equivalent of putting in place crash barriers along the road. Is there someone supportive you could be accountable to and report your progress to each week?

Beware also of the pitfalls which can be put in your way by family, friends and colleagues, who are all used to seeing you perform your old habits. If you're not careful, other people's perception of who you are can keep you 'stuck'. My clients frequently tell me stories of how colleagues can feel threatened when they try to get healthy, perhaps from fear of being left out, or not wanting to face their own need to change. You might find that some of your co-workers suddenly, perversely, become very generous with their offers to share bags of crisps and sweets!

CREATE YOUR OWN SUCCESS ADVERTISING CAMPAIGN

Advertising harnesses images and messages in order to create strong emotions. These emotions are designed to be so powerful that they can make you change your behaviour in an instant.

You can become the creative director of your own advertising campaign (aimed at you)! Looking at the long term, past the initial excitement of beginning a healthy routine, what will motivate you to stay on track? Get clear on your message: it could be an affirmation which inspires you and fires you up. For example: 'I am in control of my health, and I feel amazing.' Or 'I am creating a healthy new me. Nothing can stop me.'

Every journey towards better health is bound to be full of ups and downs. You need a strong vision you can keep reconnecting with, to keep going in the right direction. Whether that's you looking stunning and slim, turning heads as you walk down the street, or imagining yourself at 75, going about your fulfilling activities, looking 50 and enjoying life to the full. So what's *your* vision? What ad do you want playing in your mind?

VISUAL CUES

Are there visual cues which will keep you connected to your goals and give you a motivation recharge whenever you look at them? It could be a photo which you look at every day, an inspirational message written in your diary exactly one month from now, a sheet of magic whiteboard™ (a roll of static sheeting you can re-use a few times) with your key goals written on it, placed on a wall you will see every morning (while you're drying your hair or waiting for the kettle to boil), or a specific image as your screensaver.

Personally, I find the magic whiteboards very powerful. There's something about writing on the wall, and then seeing it up there every day, which keeps you focused on what matters. If I write my goals on a piece of paper, then it's likely it will just join the pile in my in-tray, and will be forgotten the next day. In my experience, we need to be reminded of our desired habits each and every day, so that they influence our choices moment by moment.

Here are seven habits you might like to be reminded of on a daily basis:

- Plan, plan, plan
- Follow the 80/20 rule
- Just keep going
- Say no with a smile
- Reconnect with my vision
- Never feel guilty
- Ask for support

I would strongly recommend you give these preparatory steps some thought, before getting started with your lifestyle change. Put the ones which appeal to you most into practice. This might mean sharing your intentions with colleagues and getting them on board. It might mean taking a day over the weekend to get your kitchen cleared and stocked up. It might also mean just being mentally prepared, with a determination to stay focused on your goals no matter what doubts and feelings of guilt come up for you in the next few weeks.

The next chapters will guide you through 31 key habits which, together will shape your new healthy lifestyle and lead to countless rewards for many years to come. Some will fall into place easily, and others you might not even be prepared to consider yet! That's okay. When you go on a journey, you wouldn't expect to reach all of your destinations at the same time, but each stage makes the next one more attainable.

So are you ready to take action? Let's move on to chapter 3.

Chapter 3

Week 1: Putting the essentials in place

 **This is not about making tough choices. It's about making easy choices consistently."**
Jeff Olson

1. Waking up to a hearty breakfast
2. Topping up the protein
3. Being carb-savvy
4. Being on good terms with fats and oils
5. Eating a rainbow of plant foods
6. Thinking fluids
7. Getting your fibre fix

HABIT 1: WAKING UP TO A HEARTY BREAKFAST

I frequently meet people who don't have breakfast, either because they don't feel hungry, or because they see this as a way of limiting the calories they eat. A good breakfast is generally accepted as a good idea, but just to muddy the waters, there have been a multitude of contradictory headlines in the press over the years - one recent study[10] hit the headlines for concluding that people's weight loss wasn't affected by whether they had breakfast or not. Apart from the fact that this was a short term study, there was no mention of *what* constituted breakfast! And there lies all the difference.

Invariably, the people I've worked with have felt much better once they've started introducing a good morning meal, even if it's a small amount at first.

Why do they feel better?

Think of breakfast as the ignition switch which sets your metabolism in motion for the day. Your ideal breakfast is nutritious and provides you with a drip feed of energy throughout the morning.

Ideally it should contain protein, especially if you're aiming to lose weight. Studies have shown that good quality protein for breakfast (such as eggs) curbed hunger during the morning much more effectively.[11]

Carbohydrates should be low glycaemic load (GL) choices like porridge or wholemeal bread (as opposed to white). The more processed a carbohydrate, the higher it will raise blood sugars – even oats can be high GL when they are cut very finely and packaged as 'instant' porridge.

> **MYTH ALERT! – All oats are good for you**
>
> Supermarket breakfast aisles and high street coffee shops are awash with oat based breakfast products. Instant porridge pots, sachets, bars, granolas and biscuits... all supposedly healthy *and* convenient. The problem is this: the more processed the oats, the more quickly they will make your blood sugars rise. They lose their principal benefit of being a 'slow release' grain! Not to mention that many of the processed oat products have had sugar or honey added to suit a sweeter tooth.

The instant porridge pots, which you can microwave for 2 minutes, are actually high in sugar. One well known brand's 'original' flavour added up to more than 22% sugar.

So what are the different forms available?

- Whole groats: the whole grain, with the husk removed. They take the longest to cook, but if you leave them to soak overnight and give them enough cooking time, you'll have a very slow release type of porridge

- Steel cut: the oat groat, cut into pieces. This is the form of oats used to make porridge in Scotland traditionally. The coarser steel cut oats are best.

- Oatmeal: ground groats, with different levels of coarseness. The smaller the grains, the higher the GL will be (because our digestive enzymes will break them down more quickly) – you're best off avoiding fine oatmeal as it will raise blood sugars faster.

- Rolled oats: the oat groats have been steamed, rolled into flakes (thickly or thinly) and toasted. The large whole flakes are less processed and low GL than the smaller fragmented flakes you get in thin-rolled oats.

Confused yet? The key thing to remember is that thick rolled oats or steel cut oats are going to have a slower release. The convenience of 'quick' oats comes at a high price!

Time Saving Tip! Too rushed to prepare porridge in the morning? Here are two ideas for you:

1. Place oats and hot water / milk / almond milk In a wide necked thermos flask before going to bed. Seal tightly. Your porridge will be nice and warm and perfectly cooked by the time you wake up.

2. Make bircher muesli instead: soak your oats overnight (in whatever liquid you use normally) along with chopped nuts and seeds – add berries or a chopped apple in the morning.

In both cases the oats benefit from being soaked overnight as this breaks down the phytic acid – a natural chemical found on grains which prevents the absorption of nutrients.

Even if you are having lower GL carbohydrates such as wholemeal or rye bread, aim to combine them with protein, as on their own, they will still cause blood sugar spikes and leave you hungry within a very short amount of time (especially if you increase the sugar content even further with marmalade or honey). A much better spread would be one of the delicious nut butters now readily available online and in some supermarkets too (check my recommended suppliers web page http://www.superwellness.co.uk/eat-well-at-work/recommended-suppliers/)

Breakfast mistakes
Speaking about blood sugars, there are a couple of common mistakes many people make, thinking they are making a healthy choice, when in fact they are setting themselves up for a blood sugar rollercoaster: the first is fruit juice and smoothies (fruit sugars in much larger quantities than you would get from eating

a whole fruit). The second mistake is to rely exclusively on fruit for breakfast, especially the higher GL types of fruit, like mango, pineapple and banana. Yes – banana! That classic 'diet' 'low calorie' breakfast actually sets you up for hunger, energy dips and eventually a slower metabolism for the rest of the day.

What if you're not hungry?

A lot of the people I work with tell me that they struggle to swallow anything first thing, often because they're not used to eating for a few hours after waking up. Their stomach is producing less hydrochloric acid in the morning (the acid which helps to break down food, especially proteins) and it can feel like food just remains on the stomach, undigested.

The answer is to gradually retrain your stomach to function as it should. Begin with small amounts of easy-to-digest food. Often I recommend protein shakes, but beware, many of these are laden with sweeteners and additives – check my recommended suppliers web page http://www.superwellness.co.uk/eat-well-at-work/recommended-suppliers/, as they take two minutes to prepare and go down easily.

Even a small handful of nuts is a good start. Make sure you chew them well though, or soak them in a little water overnight as they can be hard to digest.

Whatever works for you, as long as you manage to have at least something before leaving the house.

You could even make up a porridge or low sugar muesli and have half before you leave, and the rest when you get to work.

These same strategies can apply before going to the gym to avoid exercising on a full stomach.

So what are the top takeaways from habit 1?

- ALWAYS have breakfast

- Have something before you leave the house

- Protein for breakfast keeps hunger pangs at bay

HABIT 2: TOPPING UP THE PROTEIN

Adjusting the amount of protein you eat is probably the single change you can make with the biggest impact. You see, our modern diet, dominated by easy to come by carbohydrates, is often lacking in good quality sources of this nutrient which is so essential for the body to maintain its integrity. Missing the building blocks from protein (the amino acids), your body cries out for food and you feel that you are never satisfied, even after a large meal. 'Overweight but undernourished' is an expression that conveys this deficiency very well.

Not only does protein nourish the body, it also prevents cravings and the frustration of never quite finding the food which hits the spot.

As a rule of thumb we need approximately 1g of pure protein per Kg body weight daily, and more if exercising or pregnant (so a 70Kg person needs approximately 70g of pure protein daily). Here are a few examples as a guide:

1 tablespoon nut butter: 4g
A handful of cooked kidney beans or chickpeas(about 50g): 2g

10 almonds: 2.5g
1 tablespoon of hummus: 1g
1 cup of broccoli (about 90g): 5g
1 medium sized fillet of chicken (150g): 37g
1 medium egg: 6g

Check my online resources page to download a full list: http://www.superwellness.co.uk/eat-well-at-work/resources/

By no means do I recommend a so called 'high protein diet' (or one which might exclude carbohydrates) and people often fear that if they increased their protein intake they might suffer kidney problems or gout. The amount I recommend having, and the sources of protein (high quality lean animal and plant based) are highly unlikely to result in any such issues. On the contrary, even though some of the stories published in the press have cautioned against the 'dangers' of excess protein, there is no evidence that this is true in healthy individuals. In fact, new research is pointing towards the importance of having at least the recommended daily allowance, and preferably with each meal[12].

From my experience, every single client I have worked with, and increased the protein in their food plan, has been quite amazed by how much better they started feeling, pretty much straight away. In fact, protein is the secret weapon most people don't know about, that makes cutting out sugar so much easier.

If you remember just three things, they would be:
- Include protein in every meal
- Protein should make up around 25% of your meal
- Aim for 1g of pure protein per Kg body weight

HABIT 3: BEING CARB-SAVVY

There are plenty of nutrition and diet gurus advocating low- or no-carb diets nowadays. To a point, this is good advice, as carbohydrate foods contain varying degrees of starch, which eventually break down into sugar in the blood. The important point here is 'varying degrees' – not all carbs are created equal. In fact, rather than adopting a black and white approach of demonising carbs, it's important to avoid the ones that will cause damage, and have the right amounts of those that won't.

Some are actually beneficial, so it's essential to include them in your diet. In fact, as we mentioned in Principle #2, it's important to realise that strictly speaking, even vegetables like spinach and cabbage are classified as 'carbohydrate foods'. They are simply at the more fibre rich end of the range. More on fibre in Habit 7.

The starchier a food is, the higher its 'glycaemic index' (GI) and the more sugar it will release into your bloodstream after you've digested it. You may also come across references to 'glycaemic load' (GL), which is a bit more precise. Just as important as the amount of sugar, is the speed at which the sugar will be released. Think about it like this: if your metabolism is a fire you want to keep burning evenly, and you're using carbohydrates as a fuel to keep it burning, you'll do better with a steady supply of slow burning logs. If you throw a handful of kindling onto it (or even worse, dry straw) your fire will flare up into a very short-lived blaze, before dying down, if not dying out completely. As far as the GI of carbs is concerned, there are different factors which can affect it:

- **How refined or processed a food is**: white bread, with all fibre and substantial nutrients having been removed, dissolves very rapidly into a starchy blaze. In fact as you chew it you should already begin to taste the sweetness of the sugar being released. In the same way, consuming a food in liquid form (like fruit juice) also frees up the sugars ready to be absorbed straight through your intestinal wall directly into your blood stream.

- **How the food's been cooked:** processing food is not just the domain of food manufacturers of course. You do it in your kitchen too. And the more you process a food outside of your body, the less processing has to happen inside of your digestive system in order to free up the sugars. So porridge that's been nuked to within an inch of its life is going to release sugar much faster than porridge that's been left to soak overnight and then lightly heated for a few minutes. One of the reasons so many people like baked potatoes is that the baking process has released so much of the sweetness from the starch, making it light and fluffy. Whereas boiled or steamed potatoes, whilst still starchy, will have a lower GL. If you eat potatoes after they've cooled down, the starch will transform into something much more beneficial altogether – a 'resistant starch' with minimal release of sugar into the bloodstream, and the ability to travel much further down the digestive tract, into your bowel where it feeds beneficial bacteria .

- **What you have with it:** protein and fats help you feel fuller, so having an apple with a small handful of nuts will provide much more sustained energy and satisfaction.

- **The food's water content:** this is useful to think about when it comes to dried fruit. Although much of the volume of grapes has been reduced by removing their water content to make raisins, the sugar remains the same. Only you're more likely to get through a handful of raisins that the equivalent number of grapes (and bear in mind that grapes are a high sugar fruit as it is.)

So how do you translate all of this into daily habits?

Carbs are so ubiquitous in our diets and on your typical food outlet menu that it's useful to prioritise a few key habits:

- Aim to cut out (or start by cutting down on) all heavily refined carbohydrates and replace them by their wholemeal or wholegrain equivalent: white rice, white pasta, white bread, cereals, crisps, biscuits, cakes, chips, baked potatoes (replace with steamed new potatoes, or more nutritious sweet potatoes – still in small amounts as they are nevertheless high in starches).

- Limit starchy carbs to no more than a quarter of your meal, and always aim to roughly have a similar volume of carbs and protein. Have you seen many sandwiches where the volume of protein was equal to the volume of bread? No! You're lucky if you get a millimetre thick slice of ham or cheese in it. One way around this is to discard one half of your sandwich bread, or to choose more protein rich salads without the wrapping (chicken or tuna salad for example).

- Have some protein alongside your carbs. Even if you've switched to wholemeal toast in the morning, on its own, it won't keep your fire burning evenly. Consider having one or two eggs on top, or if that feels a bit too much for now, pick some nut spread instead (certainly in preference to jam or honey). The difference will amaze you.

- Expand your repertoire. Bread, muffins and crisps seem to be like the fuel of industry! Not a very good fuel for those who rely on them, but very good for those who sell them. Moving away from these foods is not easy because they are everywhere, and they are convenient (although I don't think the cravings they generate are convenient!). So in order to cut your reliance on these foods, you need to find others to replace them, and this might mean you try new foods, or let your taste buds get used to them. Beans, lentils and legumes are a great convenient alternative you can buy prepared and boost the contents of your salad. High protein grains like quinoa are a useful substitute, and low GL baking can open up a world of wonders (there is definitely a tasty world beyond wheat flour). For proof of this, just check the chocolate tahini cake recipe in the recipe section at the end of this book.

HABIT 4: BEING ON GOOD TERMS WITH FATS AND OILS

For the past 50 years, fat as a food group has been demonised, and wrongly so. In the 60's a scientist called Ansell Keys theorised that fat was the cause of cardiovascular disease. Even though his theory wasn't backed by any scientific studies, he proved most influential and for half a century, our whole civilisation based its eating habits on his ideas.

Much to the delight of a whole industry – the 'low fat' brigade – that flourished on the back of it. Low fat diets and low fat foods took over our food industry, like a bad virus. When you think about it now, it's just bizarre that our whole mainstream opinion about nutrition was unquestioningly that food needed to be tampered with in order to be healthy (no matter that for centuries, fat was a normal part of our diet). Somehow nature had 'mis-designed' the food chain and we needed to put it right apparently!

Unfortunately for many, although the record is gradually being set straight again, and we are realising that most fats are more beneficial than harmful, the damage has been done. Not just because so many people have followed the wrong advice, and as a result suffered deficiencies in vital nutrients, but also because the 'brainwashing' is difficult to reverse. I've seen many a client shudder at the idea of eating any type of oil at all.

Yes a more balanced view is now 'out there' and hitting the headlines. Not a day goes by it seems without a medical professional or a scientist revealing the new 'truth' about fats as, being less and less controversial, it is no longer such a risky career move to do so. And yet, it will take a lot longer for the truth to sink in. For all the official sources of information (charities and government websites) to be updated, and especially for the mind programming caused by years and years of brainwashing to be reversed.

I often meet people who have a visceral aversion to fat. Reintroducing it into their diet in healthy amounts feels truly repulsive and strange.

What's the answer?
If you feel guilty or bad about eating foods with their full fat content, or worry about the fat content in whole foods like nuts or avocados, or olive oil, then the only remedy is to be properly informed. Be aware of the reflexes you have around fats, and dispel them by seeking the most up to date evidence based information out there. And then enjoy, guilt free, the full flavour of real food, foods you might have been wrongly denying yourself for most of your life!

So what are the key fats-related daily habits to remember?
It might be scary at first, but remove from your shopping list any low fat items (yoghurts, hummus, mayonnaise, etc...) and replace them with their full fat equivalent. You might not have been aware of this, but your low fat options were mostly topped up with sugar, in order to compensate for the loss of flavour and 'mouth-feel' resulting from the removal of the fat. Having the full fat version will result in more satiety (feeling fuller for longer), less hidden sugar and therefore fewer cravings – and ultimately, a healthier relationship with food.

The only really harmful fats are those which have been processed to the degree that they've been damaged. Oils are actually a very fragile food – by this I mean that they can be easily denatured. All it takes is a bit too much heat or too much exposure to light. In fact, traditionally oil is an eminently perishable item, that gets stored for short periods and replenished often. Nowadays, I don't think most people worry about how long their sunflower oil has been hanging about in their cupboard (or on the supermarket shelf). And yet sunflower oil and vegetable oil are among the most susceptible to becoming rancid. Storing them in transparent bottles exposing them to light is a bad idea to begin with, let alone heating them to high temperatures in a frying pan. Fat molecules which have been denatured are difficult for the body to process. In places like the brain, and our cell membranes, which are made up of fat molecules from our diet, rigid trans-fats will take the place of much more fluid fat molecules, which are so much more effective at performing vital functions in the body.

What does this mean?
- Processed foods that contain vegetable oils are likely to contain these damaged fats by the very act of processing.

So avoid processed foods as much as possible (and look beyond all the marketing that might make healthy claims about it being 'natural' or 'organic')

- Equally, when you cook with the less stable fats at home, you are creating home-made trans-fats. For cooking, it's best to choose a small amount of the more stable oils and fats – the ones that are less fluid at room temperature – like coconut oil, mild olive oil (not extra virgin, as it is more fragile) or even ghee or butter.

- Ditch the processed Margarine (and disbelief inducing 'almost butter' equivalents) and go back to good old butter (leave it at room temperature to make it instantly 'spreadable'!)

Actually seek out healthy fats.
So you've got all the 'fake fats' out of your life, now what you want is to top up your levels of good healthy ones. Our definition of healthy fats is mostly 'unsaturated' fats (as long as they have been minimally and carefully processed), some of which are essential fats (the omega types). You need to actively include them, and here's a few ways you can do it:

- Use nutritious oils on your salads – cold pressed is best (less likely to have been damaged) – extra virgin olive oil, flaxseed, hemp seed. About a tablespoon for a meal. Check my recommended suppliers web page for good sources http://www.superwellness.co.uk/eat-well-at-work/recommended-suppliers/)

- Sprinkle seeds onto your meals, this works especially well for soups and salads. Raw is best, but you can also lightly toast them (not too much to avoid damaging the fats). Toasted pumpkin seeds are divine.

- Aim to have oily fish at least three times a week. Just be aware that the larger fish like tuna and swordfish have a higher mercury content too so favour smaller ones like salmon, sardines, anchovies and mackerel. Canned versions are very handy as are all the smoked and pre-cooked ones you can buy from the supermarket pre-packaged deli counter.

- Use avocados freely and with abandon: there's nothing better than a ripe avocado crushed onto a piece of rye bread as a basis for an open sandwich (with maybe some sardines on top?), or just scoop out the flesh with a teaspoon for a very quick and easy snack.

- If you haven't already, discover the delight of nut spreads – especially hazelnut and almond butters. Push the boat out and try seed spreads too, the most common of which is Tahini, a well known staple of middle-eastern recipes.

'And what about saturated fats?' I hear you ask!

We've established that butter is better than any processed substitute, so how about the saturated fats which come in dairy products and meat? And what about coconut oil? That's saturated fat too, isn't it?

Without wanting to overcomplicate things, there is a difference between the saturated fat found in bacon rind and that found in coconuts. The coconut type of saturated fat is a 'medium chain triglyceride' and the way the body deals with it, is by using it as a fuel rather than storing it. So yes, this is a type of saturated fat that gives you energy rather than padding out your thighs!

Saturated fats are a normal part of our diet, although that doesn't mean you should start gorging on butter, or finish the whole tub of ice cream every night... If you follow the 31 habits (and try the recipes) you will probably notice that you don't need to anyway. You will finally start to feel truly satisfied by the food you eat, and the need to over-indulge will fade away – and so will food related guilt.

HABIT 5: EATING A RAINBOW OF PLANT FOODS

Many people don't eat enough plant foods, and yet plants really are nature's healing dispensary. Countless studies - not to mention ancient wisdom, experience and common sense- confirm it beyond doubt. The consensus around the amount we need to stay healthy is changing, moving up to seven portions a day in the UK after many years where only five portions were recommended.

If you need motivation to increase the plant foods in your diet, here are some reasons for you:

- Plants are a rich source of vitamins and minerals, as well as a vast palette of phytochemicals (plant chemicals) which fulfil many healing roles. The reason we recommend eating 'a rainbow' is that each colour represents different types of these powerful chemicals. For example, the compounds that give green vegetables their colour are called glucosinolates. These powerful chemicals can activate enzymes which detoxify carcinogens[13] – a good reason to eat more of them!

- Plant foods are also high in fibre – and again there are many different types of fibre which the body uses in different ways (more on this in habit 7). One of its most important functions is to keep your bowels healthy and moving toxins out of your body.

- Some plant foods have been shown to help you break down fat. One study found for example that when subjects consumed capsaicin (from chillies), their fat oxidation (or breakdown) was increased. [15, 16]

- Vegetables are alkaline (their pH is above 7). Eating them loads your cells with magnesium and balances their potassium / sodium ratio, an important factor in preventing chronic illness.[17]

Why do we struggle to reach our 'fruit and veg' quotas?
A lot of people I meet have got into the habit of cramming fruit into their diets at every opportunity to increase their 'fruit and veg' quota. Fruit seems easier and more attractive to some, as they are sweet and easy to carry around as well as not needing much preparation. Some food manufacturers have jumped on the 'Five a day' bandwagon too with all kinds of over sweet alternatives which 'count as one of the five a day': dried fruit, smoothies, fruit juices, etc... Too many fruit based snacks are not ideal as they can disturb your blood sugar balance (and the liver converts fructose straight into fat[14]).

So really it's better to limit your fruit intake to maybe one or two a day and make up the rest with vegetables. Why do so many people dislike vegetables? I think partly because our food culture has mostly presented vegetables as a side show. Often overcooked, boiled to a discoloured mush, or prepared without much creativity, it's not surprising that most people would wonder what the point is and actually choose to dispense with them.

It's not just what happens to them in the kitchen that's the problem, it's what happens further upstream too. No matter where you are in the country, your local supermarket will have the same array of vegetables, and the same limited species - mostly, month in, month out. It's so boring! If only there was the same variety of tomatoes available in the supermarkets as there are breakfast cereals!

So yes, to begin with, you might have to make a conscious effort to try new vegetables and be more aware of the seasons (and when to choose veg so they are at their tastiest and most nutritious). I promise, however, that if you do, the benefits will be so great, that you will never go back. You will actually *crave* the goodness of plant foods, instead of the addictive properties of processed foods.

Here are the daily habits you can begin introducing now:
- Aim to fill half of your lunch or dinner plate with vegetables that grow above the ground (hence not starchy) and as many colours as possible.

- Aim for deeply coloured vegetables over all others as their antioxidant content will be highest (dark green leaves, rich beetroot reds, bright yellow peppers...)

- Be aware, as much as you can, of storing and preparing plant foods without losing too many nutrients. It's a good idea to eat a good proportion of them raw (50% plus) as a lot of vitamins can be damaged by heat (although not always).

- Steam or briefly stir fry vegetables rather than boiling them so you're not throwing out all the goodness with the water.

- Once chopped, vegetables begin to lose their nutrients, so try to cook them whole and cut them afterwards, and avoid chopping them too long in advance (yes those pre-chopped carrots in a bag can be handy, and if that's more convenient for you, then that's certainly a step in the right direction.)

- Get an organic box delivered every week. It can be a challenge at first, because you've got to keep on top of it, and keep coming up with ways of preparing the ever changing selection that appears on your doorstep (or on the contrary accommodating a courgette glut for a few weeks). Nowadays, delivery companies offer much more flexible ways of buying, allowing you to view your box in advance and skip the foods you don't want. You can also pick additional options from the list. So yes, you might need to make an extra effort, but the result will be a much more varied and seasonal diet of plant foods than you would have had if left to your own devices. I have a few standard recipes which accommodate pretty much any vegetable that turns up in my fridge (soups, stews and curries especially) and making a big batch over the weekend is no more time-consuming than it would have been had I made a trip to the vegetable aisle of my local supermarket.

- If you don't buy organic, then make sure you wash them well or peel them if needed. Leave them to soak in water, with a squeeze of lemon juice to cut through the sometimes oily and resistant pesticides.

Fruitful snacks – which fruit to choose?
Although mostly a good source of vitamins and other nutrients,
fruit also have a less healthy side to them: their sugar content.
At this point, a lot of people will say: 'but hang on, they are fruit
sugars! Surely that must be ok?'. Well no, not necessarily.

What's meant by 'fruit sugar' is generally fructose – a sugar molecule
which does indeed work a little bit differently in the body. Fructose
on its own doesn't raise blood sugar, that's true. What it does,
however, seems to be much worse. Biochemists have discovered
that we have a pathway in the liver which processes fructose
directly, and instead of releasing it as blood sugar (as happens with
glucose) it converts it directly into fat (fat which can remain in the
liver, around the liver, or take the form of blood lipids). So if you are
having a daily smoothie, or snacking liberally on fruit day in day out,
yes this can indeed be harmful in the long run.

Most fruit however have a blend of fructose and glucose, so some
will even cause your blood sugar to spike.

A good rule of thumb is to choose fruit which have been grown
in our temperate climate... the more sun they've been exposed to
when growing, the higher the sugar content will be. Remember also,
that having a little protein alongside lessens the cravings for further
sweet foods (apple quarters dipped in peanut butter anyone?)

So here is at a glance a list of fruit with the ideal amount for a
snack - from the most metabolically friendly to the least:

Blueberries (unlimited)
Blackberries (unlimited)
Raspberries (unlimited)
Rhubarb – unsweetened (unlimited)
Strawberries (unlimited)
Cherries (200g)
Apple (1)
Apricot (120g)
Peaches (raw or canned in natural juice) (120g)
Pear (raw or canned in natural juice) (120g)
Orange(120g)
Plums (120g)
Grapefruit (120g)
Watermelon (100g)
Kiwi (100g)
Pineapple (80g – 1 slice)
Banana (50g - half)
Dried figs (20g - 2)
Mango (50g – 1 slice)
Papaya (50g – 1 slice)
Canned lychee (30g)
Prunes – pitted (30g)
Raisins (10g - 10)
Sultanas (10g - 10)
Dried cranberries (sweetened)(10g)
Grapes (10g - 10)
Dates (8g)

HABIT 6: THINKING FLUIDS

Your brain is 75% water, so it's no wonder things start to go wrong when you don't keep it well lubricated! Dehydration is one of the biggest causes of headaches, and it also causes your brain to function less effectively. Even mild dehydration can affect your mood, your energy and your ability to concentrate and think clearly. And it doesn't take much - just 1.5% loss of fluid in the body as you go about your day can have this destructive effect.[18]

You need around 2 litres of pure, filtered water per day to stay well hydrated and if you don't, it's not just your brain that will suffer. Your body also needs sufficient moisture to digest and excrete your food. Dehydration leads to dry stools and constipation, as your body reabsorbs fluid from the bowel to satisfy its vital needs for water (do you really want your body to rely on such recycled water to function?)

A lot of people ask me if other fluids can count as part of these 2 litres. Whilst some nutritional therapists are quite adamant that only pure water counts, I am a little bit more flexible in my definition. Because, yes, there are other ways of getting water into your body and they all count. If you eat a lot of raw vegetables, then they undoubtedly have a high water content (and what's more, water bathed in plant nutrients!) If you drink a cup of tea, then yes, you are taking in fluids. The only caveat here is that some beverages like coffee, tea and soft drinks also have a diuretic effect, so you will be peeing more and losing some of the fluid you gained.

So how can you form a healthy drinking habit?

- Start the day with a big boost to your water intake: take a cup of water (warm or cold) with or without a squeeze of lemon. Increase this to a pint when you're ready.

- Think about ways you could be constantly reminded to take a sip of water at work: you could keep a pint glass on your desk, or a jug and a glass, or make a point of carrying a BPA free bottle with you when you're out and about.

- If plain water 'sticks in your throat' (as some clients have described it, while pulling a disgusted face and lifting their hand to their throat!) then there are ways to make it go down more pleasantly:
    o Slice up oranges, lemons and limes (after scrubbing their skins well) and add them to your jug of water. Slices of cucumber, or mint leaves work well too. Cordials are usually not a good idea, because they contain sugar or even worse, artificial sweeteners. There are however some healthy versions – check my recommended suppliers web page for suggestions: http://www.superwellness.co.uk/eat-well-at-work/recommended-suppliers/
    o Drink your water hot, or warm (just partly boil it). You can add some chopped ginger, a squeeze of lemon or a stick of cinnamon (or all of the above)
    o Eat lots of raw or unprocessed foods with a high water content

- Drink water away from meals. Although many believe that drinking whilst eating is a good strategy for suppressing appetite and 'flushing' food down the digestive system, in fact I don't recommend it. Digestion is not just a mechanical process of flushing food down a tube! Too much water washed down with food prevents the chemical reactions which need to take place if we're to convert the food we eat into nutrients your body can use. For this reason, you should avoid drinking too close to meals, and leave a thirty minute gap between drinking and eating.

So now we've talked about timing, what's the best type of water to drink?

It's better to filter water if you can. You can use one of those counter top filters in your kitchen, and you can even buy bottles with an inbuilt filter in them now. If you're lucky enough to have a fountain of filtered water at work, then even better. Without wanting to get too detailed and picky (if you are drinking water, then that's a good start!), it's best to avoid drinking out of a plastic bottle day in day out. Plastic water bottles have been shown to leach BPA (Bisphenol-A a chemical used in plastics) and phthalates into the water, both of which are disruptors to our hormone system[19]. (check my recommended suppliers web page for BPA free bottle suggestions: http://www.superwellness.co.uk/eat-well-at-work/recommended-suppliers/)

So your pint glass is ready and waiting on your desk, water fountain primed – good stuff!

In week 3, we'll be weighing up the pros and cons of coffee and in week 4, we'll be looking into fluids of a more alcoholic variety...

HABIT 7: GETTING YOUR FIBRE FIX

Now here's an example of an adjustment you can make to your diet, which, when performed correctly, will have a bigger impact than you might have thought. Most people equate fibre with 'healthy digestion'. This is only a small part of the story, and not necessarily accurately understood at that. Some fibres are downright harmful for digestion. But more on this later.

As you might have heard, most people do not eat enough fibre. The average intake is 12.8g a day for women and 14.8g a day for men, when the recommended average intake for adults is 18g a day[20].

How much of an impact could it make to optimise your fibre intake?

You might be surprised to know how vital fibre really is. Do you like the idea of reducing your risk for developing coronary heart disease, stroke, hypertension, diabetes, obesity, and a range of gastrointestinal diseases? How about lowering your blood pressure and serum cholesterol levels and improving the way you handle blood sugar? Oh and how about enhancing weight loss (significantly)?

Well time to examine the fibre in your diet!

Are you having enough of it, and is it the right sort?

If you rely a lot on processed foods, then your diet is likely to be deficient in fibre, along with many other crucial nutrients. Bizarrely, the fibre that has been removed from foods is then sold to us, separately, as a 'health' food, in the form of bran for example. Why not eat whole foods in the first place?

In any case, bran – the outer layer of a cereal grain - is not the be all and end all of the fibre world. If anything, this insoluble fibre is rather abrasive for the intestinal tract. It's not just the texture that's the problem. Grains are covered with a protective coat of naturally toxic chemicals, some of which are called phytic acid, so you can imagine how many of those you are introducing by selecting only the outer layer of your wheat or oat grains. Phytic acid is the plant's natural defence mechanism, whose purpose it is to protect the grain as it transits through an animal's digestive tract, so that it can safely be excreted and germinate once it finds a fertile spot.

Phytic acid blocks the absorption of nutrients in our food and also blocks some of the enzymes needed for us to digest the food[21]. So it's probably not ideal for us to be sprinkling bran liberally onto breakfast every day!

The best fibre foods

There are two main families of fibre: 'non-soluble' (they go straight through without breaking down) and 'soluble' (which dissolve, providing food for your beneficial bacteria).

Granted, non-soluble fibres from grains and vegetables like cabbage or potato skin are very useful to add bulk in the bowel and push everything along, however soluble fibres (from most fruit and vegetables, oats, lentils for example) do much more than that. They provide various sources of food for the all-important gut bacteria.

We are only just beginning to understand how much our gut bacteria are responsible for (we touched on this topic in Chapter 2 – Principle #3: Digestion and Detoxification). It's not just you and the food you eat – these trillions of bugs play a vital role as an interface between the two of you, from producing vital nutrients to deciding how many calories you'll extract from your meal.

They love to feed from the inulin from onions, and the resistant starch from beans or potatoes that have gone cold.

So in conclusion, which habits will ensure you are getting your optimum fibre fix every day?

- Leave out foods that have been stripped of fibre (breakfast cereals, white bread, pasta, rice, cakes and biscuits made with white flour)

- There's no way around it: you need to get a variety of plant fibres into your diet each day. It doesn't have to be complicated:

  o opt for a salad instead of a sandwich
  o use tinned beans and lentils for quick salads
  o have porridge made with whole oats for breakfast (with some ground flaxseeds on top)
  o leave grains (including rice, quinoa and oats), lentils and pulses to soak for at least a few hours before preparing them, to break down the phytic acid
  o if you like potatoes, have them cold in potato salads to give your gut bacteria the benefit of resistant starch (the form potato starch takes when cold, instead of dissolving into glucose)
  o have a piece of fruit whole instead of a smoothie or juice

Chapter 4

Week 2: Getting into a routine

 **Our brains and our abilities
are like muscles. They can be
strengthened with practice."**
Chip Heath and Dan Heath

8. De-sugarizing
9. Planning to succeed
10. Managing supplies
11. Diarizing healthy habits
12. Storing and prepping food at work
13. Mastering the art of home-made lunches
14. Exercising smart

HABIT 8: DE-SUGARIZING
There is no doubt about it: sugar is addictive. In fact studies
carried out on rats showed that when given the choice between
sugar water on the one hand and cocaine and heroin on the other
(having been exposed to them before), they chose the sugar. 94%
of the time[23].

Sugar stimulates the reward pathways in the brain, so cutting
down can cause some withdrawal pangs for a few days, but is
an essential step towards good health and a trimmer waistline.
Professor Lustig, a paediatrician who specialises in treating

overweight children in San Francisco, has spent 16 years studying the effects of sugar on the central nervous system, metabolism and disease. His book, 'Fat Chance: The Bitter Truth About Sugar' exposes the direct link between sugar and obesity.

A lot of people say to me: 'I don't have much sugar in my diet', but then, when we look at their food diary, it becomes clear that in fact, they are having much more than their body can deal with. This is because most people, when they think of sugar, think of the teaspoons you add to your tea or coffee, or the sugar you sprinkle onto your cornflakes in the morning. I remember growing up, it was perfectly normal to sprinkle sugar onto fruit!

If you don't do any of those things, well that's a start. However there are many more sources of sugar, some of which are not obvious at all at first sight: if you've replaced sugar with raisins or honey, unfortunately, the end result is still the same: these 'natural sweeteners' have much the same negative impact on your metabolism, disrupt the environment in your digestive tracts and keep stimulating the reward centres of the brain, keeping you addicted to the sweetness.

Hidden sugar
Of course, there are sweet foods, like cake, biscuits and desserts, but there are also many so called savoury foods now which are high in sugar. Ketchup typically contains 25% sugar! Many processed foods have high levels too. Most breakfast mueslis and granolas, even though they look healthy (whatever that means!), have extremely high levels, as do cereal bars – often upwards of 25%.

The only way forward really, is to gradually cut these foods out, and the first step might just be to become more aware of the sugar content in foods. I always check the labels of anything I buy. It might seem time consuming at first, but it is an eye opener, and gradually if you do the same, your awareness of what you put into your body will become more acute. I look for the amount of sugar per 100g (it should never really be more than 10%) and I also look at the ingredients list to spot how high up the list sugar appears (and sometimes it appears many times, in different guises:

Sugar in disguise
- Maltodextrin
- Dextrose
- Cane syrup
- Honey
- Concentrated fruit
- Apple juice
- Glucose syrup
- Maltose
- Fructose
- Natural sweetener

In some ways, there is no completely pain-free way to cut down on sugar. Yes you will probably miss it in the first few days and you are even likely to feel withdrawal symptoms. You might feel tired, exhausted even, struggle to sleep and feel in a bad mood. Unfortunately, this is what sugar sets you up for, and why in the long run you are so much better off without it. So my advice is to bite the bullet, and be prepared. It might not even be that bad – some of my clients start feeling better instantly.

So what are the daily habits you can put in place to help you 'de-sugarize'?

- There is a secret to minimise the sugar withdrawal symptoms, and that's making sure you maximise your intake of nutritious foods: protein especially, but also good fats and vitamin rich foods. By giving your body the nutrients it needs, it is less likely to crave empty calories and quick rewards.

- If you do add sugar to your drinks or food, begin to reduce it gradually (go from two teaspoons to one, from one to a half, etc...)

- Check labels on all of the food you buy (sugar should be minimal in savoury foods, and ideally no more than 10g per 100g in sweet foods). Don't be fooled by sugar in disguise If you are addicted to the sweet taste, try using natural low glycaemic load sweeteners like xylitol or stevia (check my website for a list of suppliers http://www.superwellness.co.uk/eat-well-at-work/recommended-suppliers/), but bear in mind that the end game is to get rid of the sweet tooth altogether.

- Remember that your taste buds last just ten days before they are replaced, so although you might miss the taste initially, very soon, the foods you were used to will begin to taste oversweet, and, quite frankly, disgusting!

- Swap milk chocolate for dark – the darker, the better. Still check the labels though, you'd be surprised how many dark chocolates are still high in sugar (check my website for a list of suppliers http://www.superwellness.co.uk/eat-well-at-work/recommended-suppliers/).

- Aim for one or two pieces of fruit a day maximum, but really top up your vegetable levels

- Steer clear of fake health foods: dried fruit, fruit smoothies, fruit juice, cereal bars, high sugar granolas and mueslis

- Replace high sugar sauces like ketchup with alternatives like Tabasco sauce, hummus, spices, lemon juice and herbs.

- Replace ready-made salad dressing with home-made (see box for recipe)

- Steer clear of syrups (added into coffees) or fancy 'balsamic glaze' packed full of sugar to make it sticky.

Easy home-made salad dressing
1 teaspoon mustard (Dijon or other)
3 tablespoons balsamic vinegar
8 tablespoons extra virgin olive oil
1 clove garlic (roughly crushed to release the juices)
Add all of the ingredients into a container with a tight lid
Shake well and use (and store in the fridge)

HABIT 9: PLANNING TO SUCCEED

You've probably heard or even used the saying: 'If you fail to plan, you plan to fail.'

Well in no area is this truer than in your daily eating habits.

Think about it. We eat at least three times a day (plus snacks), seven days a week, at regular intervals. This is quite a major logistics operation, and we often underestimate the effort involved.

I've heard lots of people justify a lack of planning by a lack of time, but this is a very poor excuse. In fact, spending 10 or 15 minutes planning once a week would save huge amounts of time – all those accumulated hours spent queuing at the sandwich place, deciding, hesitating... those last minute stops at the shop on your way home, not to mention all the mental energy spent wondering what to make with what you've got in the fridge. And then there's all the avoidable pitfalls a lack of planning sets you up for: visits to the snack machine, the petrol station, fast food outlets. With guilt as an extra bonus. You get the picture.

Nine times out of ten, the people I work with start by underestimating the value of planning. I think it's just human nature. You think: 'Bah, I'll be fine, I know what I'm doing' and it might even seem like sitting down to actually write down what you're going to have the following week is a little bit 'overkill'.

Trust me, it isn't.

And invariably after two or three weeks of struggling to stick with this regime, people realise just what a lifesaver planning really is, and that if they don't do it, yes they really will fail, and end up going back to old habits.

So how can you get this planning habit underway?
- I recommend using a meal planning template with an area to do your shopping list on the same page (visit my website

to download one for free in the resources area http://www.superwellness.co.uk/eat-well-at-work/resources/)

- Stick with the same time each week for planning, for example Friday evening (unless your work schedule is very irregular and say, you work shifts)

- Keep it simple, it doesn't have to be a big task (this will only make you put it off!) It shouldn't take more than 10 or 15 minutes.

- Use your diary alongside, so you can plan for meals out, travelling, or particularly busy days.

- Gradually build up a repertoire of easy, tasty and quick recipe ideas (see the recipe section at the end of this book) and use this mainly. Try at least a couple of new recipes each month so you can keep it varied (Check my website for healthy recipe book suggestions http://www.superwellness.co.uk/eat-well-at-work/resources/)

- Make it easy: recipes are nice to bring in new ideas and keep it interesting, but there is no harm in also having meals where you just have a piece of grilled fish or meat, and steam whatever vegetables you have alongside it. Variety is good, but don't become obsessed with change. Having the same lunch two or three times in a row is fine, as long as it's nutritious, and you're happy with it.

- Plan time for shopping, and also preparing food. The weekend is often a good time to cook in bulk and store away your home made 'takeaways' in the freezer for a week night.

And it's not just stews and soups that can be prepared in this way. You can prepare individual portions of brown rice, quinoa, or breakfast oat pancakes (see recipe section) which can then be heated in the toaster on a work morning.

HABIT 10: MANAGING SUPPLIES

If you want to stick with your healthy new habits, it's essential you have a strategy for keeping stocked up without stress or waste of time. Of course, doing a meal plan helps enormously with this. Knowing what you need in advance will save you time and money when you hit the shops.

Shopping online of course saves a lot of time, and it doesn't just have to be from your supermarket. The beauty of it is that you can place a weekly order for all your staple foods, which you hardly have to spend any time on at all.

Do question whether your supermarket is your only option too. There are others, which you might find are more cost effective, time-efficient, or even closer aligned with your ethical ideals.

Personally I find that buying my vegetables and other fresh produce from an organic delivery service takes away a lot of the need for supermarket shopping, and makes me use a wider variety of foods, but yes, you do need to be prepared to stay on top of this weekly influx and ideally time the delivery so that you'll have time to bulk prepare soups and stews with the produce.

Probably less widely known are places where you can buy food (and other supplies) in bulk, saving money and lots of store visits. There are a couple of suppliers in the UK specialising in healthy or organic foods, which normally supply businesses. It's possible however to get together with other people and make it worthwhile ordering the quantities they require.

We order weeks or even months worth of supplies for our store cupboard staples, like rice, quinoa, nut butters, tamari sauce, bouillon powder, and even chemical free washing powder and soap. Check my website for these suppliers details: http://www. superwellness.co.uk/eat-well-at-work/recommended-suppliers/

The small trickle of supplies we need each day adds up to one big river of cash if you add it up throughout the year. Choosing your suppliers isn't just a matter of convenience, but also an ethical choice you're making as a consumer, so it's worth taking a step back and thinking twice about how you vote with your cash.

So what can you do now to get organised with your supplies?
- Try to bulk buy as much as possible of your staple foods and other things too, providing you have the storage to do so. Getting together with friends or colleagues to buy and share supplies together can be a good motivation to try new things.

- Think creatively and make use of the wealth of online suppliers available. Try to automate your food purchases as much as you can.

- Keep supplies in strategic places, where they'll be needed. If you suffer from afternoon dips, keep healthy snacks in your work drawer, keep some essentials in the fridge at work (if available), have dry snacks to hand in your car.

- Have an emergency supply in your cupboard for times when supplies run low: tinned beans (not high sugar content baked beans though!), tinned fish, oat cakes, nut butter, you can even buy individual portions of pre-cooked lentils and quinoa now. Not the cheapest way but probably the quickest – just open, empty, et voila!

HABIT 11: DIARIZING HEALTHY HABITS

Just as you schedule time in your diary for work and social activities, you can and should do the same for your health and wellbeing. The reason it might seem a bit outlandish is that so many people believe that making time for themselves is indulgent – let alone actually planning it!

The thing is, if you don't protect that time, it's very unlikely to happen. There will always be other demands (usually from other people) which will seem to take priority.

Yes, this can require a shift in mindset initially, but it's worth it. Believe me, it's the best investment in time you can make, and 20 years from now, which will you value most? The hour you spent exercising (and keeping diabetes at bay) or the email you decided at the last minute was more important?

Your body and mind are your irreplaceable engines of success. Unless you give them regular attention, they will begin to let you down, and those work activities that seemed so important will seem futile in comparison.

It's worth taking a step back and evaluating what your true priorities are. Are you thinking of your long term wellbeing, or is your head buried in the sand? Also, purely from an effectiveness point of view, your wellness routine doesn't have to be chaotic because of a busy schedule, it should really be a part of the schedule!

So how do you begin to make time in your diary for healthy habits, when you're confronted with back to back meetings, hours of commuting, and a demanding boss?

- Make a clean break. All too often, people spend their lunch hour (or half hour) at their desk. Although you might be on a slightly more relaxed mode, you're still very much in a work mindset. Going for a short walk or sitting in the park for ten minutes will break up the day and reboot your brain.

- Schedule exercise in your diary. Even more effective is to involve other people – a trainer or an exercise buddy, who are counting on you to turn up.

- Even scheduling relaxation, as self-indulgent as it may seem to you, is important, and even essential, if you are someone who struggles to switch off. For a start, planning holidays in advance is a very good idea (especially if you are self-employed like me – I would never leave my desk if I didn't plan breaks away!). There are other regular relaxing routines you might consider putting in your diary. A monthly massage, regular relaxing social get-togethers, daily breathing exercises or meditation are very helpful too.

- With regard to food, meal planning is essential, and as mentioned before, ideally, it should be in your diary at the same time each week. You may also want to schedule in shopping, or a big cook up.

- Use those handy calendar reminders to help you reinforce habits too. Do you forget to drink water? Set yourself a morning reminder to pop by the water fountain. Some people I know even struggle sometimes to remember to stop and have lunch!

HABIT 12: STORING AND PREPPING FOOD AT WORK

If you are lucky enough to have a good restaurant or canteen in your workplace, that provides real healthy food, this can save you a lot of time and energy. Make the most of it! I have come across workplace catering providers who are really raising the standards in this area, offering employees locally sourced ingredients, prepared and cooked entirely on the premises. Their facilities and menu were on a par with the best restaurants in town. At a fraction of the price. In this case, you'd be mad not to take advantage of such an opportunity.

If you are left to your devices, then going out to buy food every day can be time consuming, not to mention expensive! And let's face it, preparing food at home is not always going to happen. So if you have access to a kitchen at work, then here are some tips to make full use of it.

When you do your weekly shop, include your 'work shop' – a bag of food you can bring into work and store away for the week. This might include dry foods you can keep in your locker, or desk – healthy granola, oatcakes, tinned fish – and fresh foods that will last two or three days in the fridge. I always used to find myself taking in a bag of prepared salad, cherry tomatoes, hummus, feta cheese, olives, maybe an avocado or two, and as protein, packaged fish – smoked salmon or mackerel for example. Meat eaters might also bring cold meats or chicken from the deli counter.

I know not everyone has the luxury of a kitchen at work though, so in the next 'habit' I'll share a couple of ideas for alternatives.

HABIT 13: MASTERING THE ART OF HOME-MADE LUNCHES

Bringing your own lunch into work puts you in control of the ingredients you choose, and once you have a 'system' in place for doing this, it becomes an amazing time saving option too. Just think about it: how much time do you spend queuing up at the local deli? How much energy do you waste wondering what to have each day, especially once you get to the point of being really hungry and particularly open to temptation from all kinds of pastry based options! Just think of all the mental energy wasted on the internal battle that then goes on between good intentions and evil temptations. Here are a few options for your homemade lunch 'system':

- Ready to assemble: you don't even need to spend time making lunch at home, you can just bring in the various elements of your lunch, store them in your fridge at work if you have one, and just throw them together on a plate. Ready sliced cuts of meat and smoked fish lend themselves very well to this option, along with bagged salads, pots of hummus and conveniently packaged oatcakes or slices of rye bread.

- Last night's leftovers: always think of cooking extra quantities for dinner, and then simply storing what's left into a Tupperware to take to work. If you need to reheat it, then just make sure you transfer it into a glass or ceramic bowl first, to avoid chemicals leaching out into the food. Otherwise, for stews and soups, wide necked flasks are very handy – no need to heat anything up, and even more time saved!

- Made especially: if you have time over the weekend, then you could make a batch of food to last you two or three lunches (see the recipe section for ideas)

- If you don't have the luxury of a kitchen or a fridge at work, there is a way around this too. I often find myself on site at a client's office with very little time to get food for lunch (and certainly no fridge to store a salad in) so I bring my trusty food flask. This type of wide necked flask can be filled with hot food first thing, and it will keep it warm until lunchtime. A spoon is usually embedded into the lid, so all you have to do is unscrew and eat a lovely home-made stew or soup. Very comforting.

HABIT 14: EXERCISING SMART

Hand in hand with eating well at work goes exercising smart. In fact, exercise is often the first thing that springs to mind when people think about wellness at work – on-site classes, subsidised gyms, pedometer based challenges... and nutrition often gets ignored!

The truth is you cannot substitute one for the other. You can't replace physical movement with more quinoa in your diet, and at the same time, spending hours in the gym each day is not going to make up for poor nutrition. And yet I've heard people utter this belief so many times! 'I've spent 45 minutes on the treadmill, so I deserve a treat' (they say, reaching for a very large and sticky muffin).

Sound familiar? It's a hard wired equation in most people's minds: burn calories, make room for more. Unfortunately based on an over-simplification, as the food you eat is affecting your metabolism on many different levels (as mentioned in Chapter 1)... but I digress.

Hopefully, if you've always focussed exclusively on exercise as the key to good health, reading this book will offer you insights into ways that you can get the most out of your training thanks to a few diet adjustments. Now if you're someone who shuns exercise like the plague, I'm hoping that reading this section will give you the impetus to get started with some achievable goals, however small they may be, that will make a considerable difference down the line.

Whatever your relationship is to exercise, as ever, my aim is to highlight ways that you can *optimise* whatever you are doing and ultimately fulfil more of your personal potential in spite of time and practical limitations.

Where to begin?

There are so many theories around about the best forms of exercise – it can get very confusing (as with nutrition!). The bottom line seems to be that, whatever form of exercise appeals to you, anything that gets you moving is a good place to start. Then working up from there, yes, there are specific benefits to specific methods of exercise, and some are more effective than others. If you are the sort of person who likes to squeeze the most benefit out of every minute of exercise you do, there are certain forms which give you 'more bang for your buck' – I'll come to this in a minute.

Simply moving

There's been extensive research in recent years highlighting the damage caused by sedentary behaviour[24]. Any period of time upwards of 2 hours with no movement begins to affect our fitness levels, with serious consequences. So serious in fact that prolonged sitting has been dubbed 'the new smoking'. It is associated with higher cholesterol levels and greater waist circumference, which in turn can lead to cardiovascular and metabolic disease. Slack muscles do not contract to effectively pump blood to the heart. Blood can pool in the legs and the function of arteries begins to deteriorate. Lovely.

So if you sit at a desk for hours on end, integrating just a few extra minutes of walking into your day could bring considerable benefits. In fact, one study showed that short, easy five minute walks made a significant difference. Three of these are enough to reverse the damage to leg arteries caused by three hours of sitting[25].

Taking a stroll after eating

While we're on the subject of walking, a crucial time when it's beneficial is after eating. Research has shown that a simple 15 minute post meal stroll makes a significant contribution to your body's ability to control blood sugars[26]. If you remember what we covered in Chapter 1, you'll know that blood sugars usually call for insulin to control them, and insulin in turn switches on the fat stores... so 15 minutes of walking after lunch might be a more intelligent way of approaching your exercise routine than 45 minutes on the treadmill with the aim of burning calories.

The real engine of health: muscle

Now of course, moving more throughout the day, that's a step in the right direction. But ultimately it's not really enough. If you truly believe you deserve an optimum level of fitness and health, then yes, you need to build more and different forms of exercise into your week.

And recent research has dispelled quite a few myths around the most effective approaches. You might be surprised if I tell you that there are much more effective ways of burning fat for example than long, low intensity cardiovascular workouts. The main discovery which has been made in recent years is just how important muscle is to our wellbeing, our health *and* our ability to control body weight. Beginning with this understanding can revolutionise your whole approach to exercise, not to mention the results you achieve.

Gradual decline

As we get older, we naturally lose muscle – around five percent every 10 years from age 30 onwards. This gradual and insidious process undermines our general health (metabolism, bone strength, cardiovascular health, and more) so that when we get to age 60, 70 or 80, suddenly the degeneration becomes noticeable. One day you find yourself struggling to get out of your chair! And in the meantime, this programmed decline affects how you feel day to day, your energy levels and your risk factors for developing chronic illness. This is why it's so important to maintain, and even better, increase your muscle strength as early as possible.

Keep in mind that your muscle tissue is the place where your cells are most capable of producing energy. Each muscle cell contains hundreds of mitochondria – the 'dynamos' that convert fuel into energy. Exercising muscle increases mitochondria numbers and athletes will have around 4,000 per muscle cell. What this means? A more effective metabolism and the bottom line is a better ability to burn fat. Even while you're sleeping!

Resistance training

For these reasons, resistance training, or activity which causes the muscles to work, should be at the top of your priority list for exercise. Some good examples would be swimming, weights, yoga and pilates and other exercises where you use your own body weight like squats or planks. By increasing your strength, you'll achieve far wider ranging benefits than say, just focusing on cardiovascular work, counterintuitive as this might seem in our treadmill culture.

High intensity

If you want to take resistance exercise to its most effective expression, I'd recommend you seriously look into 'high intensity resistance training', which allows the body to draw the maximum benefit from sessions of just 12 minutes a week!

The benefits are quite astounding (and thoroughly researched) – firstly the fact that given a high enough weight level, two minutes on one exercise is sufficient to stimulate rapid strength increase. This in turn conditions the rest of the body, particularly organs like the heart and the lungs, which have to adapt to a higher demand in blood flow and oxygen. This type of training is also unique in the way it taps muscle fibres and depletes glycogen stores in a way an ordinary gym session wouldn't. This makes it particularly good for improving insulin sensitivity and particularly beneficial in conditions linked to insulin resistance and problems regulating to blood glucose control.

In fact, it has been shown to increase glucose uptake in the cells by 23 percent after only four months. The brilliant book full of peer reviewed references "Body by Science" by Doug McGuff and John Little[27] is a good place to read up on it, or ask a well informed exercise expert to guide you through this routine.

The results this approach can achieve are so impressive that I now systematically use it alongside nutrition in order to achieve rapid progress with my clients – especially those whose diaries don't allow much time for exercise. In fact I've teamed up Dr Masood, a Medical Doctor specialising in insulin receptor resistance and metabolic problems, to launch a dedicated facility called Rev5 providing this type of training in Windsor, Berkshire. You can read more about the research and our own client case studies at www.rev5.co.uk

Interval training

Another form of high intensity training which is well researched, interval training will really supercharge your exercise routine whilst saving precious time. One of the reasons it's so effective is that it triggers the release of human growth hormones (HGH), sometimes referred to as the 'fitness hormone'. Much as with muscle tissue, levels begin to decline after we reach the age of 30, contributing to the ageing process.

By doing short bursts of effort, interspersed with slower paced intervals, you can increase HGH by as much as 771 percent (!) within eight weeks. One study on a particular interval training protocol called Sprint 8 showed that middle aged workers who practised Sprint 8 for eight weeks lost on average 31 percent of their body fat[28]. And this was just doing sessions of a few minutes, no more than three times a week.

With this intense form of exercise, I would recommend asking a personal trainer to design a programme for you, based on your fitness level, which you can gradually build up.

So that's the theory, now how can you put all of this into practice?

- Start simple: if you don't exercise at all, then taking two or three five minute walks a day will be beneficial. One of our participants in the corporate nutrition challenges we run told us she set her timer on her phone to beep once every 90 minutes, prompting her to take a five minute walk. She says this simple step has made a huge difference to her energy levels and helped her lose weight easily.

- If time is tight, then think of ways you could fit exercise into your day: getting off a stop early on public transport and walking the rest of the way, avoiding the lift in favour of stairs or walking over to speak to colleagues instead of emailing. One of my clients set herself an easy goal of walking up all the stairs in her work building at least once a day (there were four floors) – a pretty good weekly workout when you add it all up!

- Use your lunch break wisely by going for a walk after eating, instead of staying in front of your screen – you'll be tuning your engine and getting much more mileage per gallon (energy from your food!)

- Optimise. You don't have to spend hours in the gym to maximise your fitness potential. If done correctly, high intensity resistance and interval training are far more effective ways of achieving results, in a matter of minutes.

- Finally, as with your nutrition, start as you mean to continue. The aim is to build fitness activities into your routine for the long term. And you're more likely to stick with habits which fit in with your life and bring you the most reward for an achievable amount of effort.

Chapter 5

Week 3: travelling and rushing to meetings

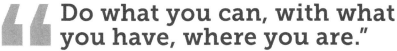 **Do what you can, with what you have, where you are."**
Theodore Roosevelt

15. Having a healthy coffee strategy
16. Making hotel breakfasts work for you
17. Choosing well in the sandwich shop
18. What to eat when there's no time
19. Great snacks for the road
20. Dancing with stress
21. Relaxing and chewing

HABIT 15: HAVING A HEALTHY COFFEE STRATEGY

Coffee can be a sensitive subject. Many people who work long and intense hours see it as a necessary part of their day, essential fuel to keep them productive and sharpen their thinking.

I must admit, it's one the habits I've found most deeply ingrained in myself, I love the taste and smell of coffee and when you work from a home office as I do much of the time, nipping down to the coffee shop for a change of scenery can be hard to resist. Especially with coffee shops equipped with plug sockets and comfy armchairs – taking your laptop down for a couple of hours away from any interruptions seems like a bit of a win-win.

Is it really though?

Coffee is also one of the most controversial areas in nutrition, with seemingly contradictory research conclusions. The truth is, our ability to metabolise coffee is a very individual thing. Recent research has shown that individuals have variations on the genes involved in caffeine metabolism, so that our tolerance thresholds can be very variable[29].

From my personal experience, the effects of caffeine are very clear. Any caffeine after 2pm, and I know I stand no chance of sleeping that night! If I have more than one small cup, I begin to feel jittery and 'on edge', and even with a small coffee a day more than three days in a row, my levels of anxiety start to increase noticeably. I suspect my tolerance levels are very low.

So although there are numerous studies linking caffeine to benefits from helping prevent Alzheimer's disease to reducing the risk of certain cancers, it doesn't mean that drinking 6 cups of coffee a day is necessarily a good idea. As mentioned earlier, the effect of caffeine on the body is very individual and it always makes sense to listen to your own body.

One of my clients, who was worried about his increasing blood pressure, was drinking up to six cups of coffee a day, thinking this was fine because one observational study connected coffee drinking with a lower mortality rate. When I did manage to persuade him to try lowering his coffee intake, he immediately started to feel better and his blood pressure came down too. He ended up giving up completely!

Another concern is the impact of caffeine on your stress hormones. Raised cortisol levels cause blood sugar levels to increase, only leading to more fat storage around the midriff. As a stimulant, it perpetuates the blood sugar rollercoaster with all the cravings that arise in the 'down' stages. So although the caffeine induced adrenaline mobilises your brain and energy in the short term, this is not natural energy from normal metabolism; over time, it's actually *taxing* your body's ability to produce energy naturally – there are no quick fixes without downsides it seems!

Of course the same goes for other drinks containing caffeine. If you have more than two cups of tea a day, then levels will start to build up, and the worst offenders are colas and 'energy drinks' which combine the blood sugar disrupting effects of sugar and caffeine and sometimes also the toxic effects of artificial sweeteners as well.

So what steps can you take to optimise your caffeine strategy?
- Listen to your body. If you feel jittery after more than one cup of coffee, then I would recommend reducing your intake, if not eliminating coffee completely.

- If you are ready to reduce caffeine, then it's best to do so gradually, as those who go cold turkey often suffer quite severe withdrawal symptoms from headaches to cold sweats! You could start by replacing some of your caffeine drinks with a decaffeinated version, or even better, a different drink with beneficial properties: green, white or red bush tea are all great sources of antioxidants, which protect the body from damaging free radicals (check my website for suppliers http://www.superwellness.co.uk/eat-well-at-work/recommended-suppliers/)

- Be cautious about strongly increasing your intake of 'decaf' drinks as most decaffeination processes involve chemical solvents such as methylene chloride or ethyl acetate, which can be very toxic. It's worth seeking out coffee which has been decaffeinated using the 'Swiss Water Process' instead. (check my website for suppliers http://www.superwellness. co.uk/eat-well-at-work/recommended-suppliers/)

HABIT 16: MAKING HOTEL BREAKFASTS WORK FOR YOU

Travelling for work doesn't mean your healthy intentions are doomed. In fact, most places now make it a breeze to stick to a great eating plan whilst dining out and staying in hotels. Of course, being on the road disrupts your routine, it forces you to think about your options and make a conscious decision when faced with more temptations – that's the challenge. But on the upside, there are usually plenty of healthy and tasty alternatives to choose from.

Hotel breakfasts are usually a doddle, because in the UK at least, you mostly have the option of a cooked breakfast, with good amounts of protein to set you up for the day. So you get a great nutritious and filling breakfast without the hassle – let's face it, you probably wouldn't normally have time during the week to prepare a cooked breakfast!

Naturally, side step all the pitfalls, as you would at home: walk straight past the fruit juice dispenser, be wary of the cereal jars: muesli is often laden with sugar, especially if it contains lots of raisins and dried fruit (which you can pick out!).

Sometimes of course, you might find yourself with very little choice. I'll always remember a hotel I stayed at in Colorado. The breakfast buffet included a large plate full of pop tarts (33% sugar), pastries and, thankfully, a glass bowl full of hard boiled eggs. Even if the breakfast you end up having is not perfect, then it's worth remembering, you can only do the best you can with what is available to you.

HABIT 17: CHOOSING WELL IN THE SANDWICH SHOP

In most towns, the selection of stores catering for lunch is very similar, and offers so much more choice than was available a few years ago.

I was even surprised recently at the healthy choice available at an exhibition I was visiting: quinoa and feta cheese salad, packed full of spinach leaves, with the most delicious lemon dressing. Impressive! I had been expecting the usual selection of ham and cheese sandwiches.

These days, you're likely to find delicious Japanese teriyaki soup, or nutritious frittata, not to mention tasty salads, including a good share of protein and lots of plant foods. It's not generally too difficult to pick something delicious and healthy on the go.

If you do happen to be in the middle of nowhere, with nothing but a garage selling sandwiches, then make sure you pick one with as generous a protein filling as is available, and try discarding one side of the bread to lower your lunch's glycaemic load.

Check the resources page on my website for a list of the best choices from different high street food outlets http://www. superwellness.co.uk/eat-well-at-work/resources/.

HABIT 18: WHAT TO EAT WHEN THERE'S NO TIME

I've often worked with clients who said that finding any time at all to eat was a challenge. Whether you work in a public facing job, like on a shop floor, or are 'on duty' all day, training clients for example, there are situations where you can find yourself with very limited facilities for storing and even eating food. If you're lucky enough to have food made available to you, the choice on offer is out of your control. So what can you do in these situations?

The first thing to remember is that you can't be a paragon of nutritional perfection all the time – sometimes you've just got to do the best you can with the options available! So here are a few suggestions for you:

The pick of the sandwich platter

Meeting catering is often heavily biased towards bread, pastry and generally high GL foods, with low protein and fresh plant foods in proportion – brown foods as my sister calls them. Given the choice, it's best to avoid any pastry and crisps completely and pick sandwiches made with brown bread, and containing protein (there's usually an egg or chicken option).

If you're lucky enough to have fresh crudités sticks with hummus served alongside the sandwiches, then make a beeline for those.

Take your own snacks

I often run day long drop-in clinics for corporate clients, where I see people back to back all morning and all afternoon with a very short lunch break, and no time to even begin thinking about searching for something to buy. On these occasions, I make sure firstly that I have a really good breakfast, sometimes adding a clean protein shake (by clean, I mean one which doesn't contain all the additives all too often found in commercial protein powders) to my normal breakfast. I also make sure I've got a good stock of dry, nourishing snacks to keep me going. I sometimes make up some extra protein shake and take it with me in a flask – there's nothing easier than sipping on a protein shake, even while you're in the middle of a meeting.

Some of the things I take include: nuts, mixed in with a couple of dried fruit or a piece of fresh fruit, seed mixes, packaged snacks like bounce balls are also very good. There are also some delicious cacao cinnamon kale chips available now, which are very low in sugar and high in protein and nutrients. Just beware of green bits in your teeth! Check my website for suppliers http://www.superwellness.co.uk/eat-well-at-work/recommended-suppliers/)

Home-made snacks that don't need a fridge
If you regularly find yourself in work situations where you need to eat on the fly, ideally you don't want to have to rely on ready-made, shop bought snacks every day. So you probably need to explore some other options that are going to be better for you long term. Nowadays, I rely heavily on food flasks when I'm in those situations.

A wide-necked food flask is inexpensive and easy to carry around – it's ideal for stews and soups, which you can heat up in the morning. It will keep your food hot until lunchtime, and you can find models which have a spoon embedded in the lid. There's nothing quite like this home comfort in the middle of a hectic day. Check my website for suppliers http://www.superwellness.co.uk/eat-well-at-work/recommended-suppliers/)

Avocados are also a favourite of mine for a fresh portable food that will only require a penknife and a spoon (and maybe a paper napkin).

On the road

The ultimate challenge for sticking to a healthy eating programme is for people who are constantly on the road as part of the job they do. What can you do when the car, van or lorry is your office?

Perhaps you need to think about a more permanent solution to address this – like a cool box in the boot, filled with some hassle free staples you can top up when convenient. When you find yourself in the supermarket or a food outlet with some good choices, stock up!

I've come across dedicated individuals who carried in the boot of their car a juicer they could use to stick to their very healthy lifestyle while touring the country delivering seminars. If you are on the road more often than at home, perhaps even staying several nights in the same location, then it's worth considering taking an extractor with you such as Nutribullet – easy to use and clean, and doesn't take up much space.

HABIT 19: GREAT SNACKS FOR THE ROAD

A common belief is that you shouldn't eat between meals. In fact, snacking doesn't have to be a bad thing. On the contrary, when you are cutting out sugar and getting your blood sugars into balance, well-chosen snacks mid-morning and mid-afternoon keep your metabolism running smoothly. They prevent energy dips, hunger pangs and cravings and keep you safe from the temptations of high sugar foods, which seem so appealing when blood sugars are low!

Once your blood sugars are more even (it can take a few days, or sometimes a few weeks, depending on how focused you are) then you might find that you don't actually need the snacks any longer. Some of my clients say they are eating so much more nutritious food with their meals that they only need one of the snacks, if any at all. As long as they don't approach the next meal ravenous, then that's absolutely fine.

So what are the best portable snacks? The hallmark of a good snack is a high protein and low sugar content. So that rules out vast swathes of the snack market: chocolate bars, you might have guessed that! But certainly most cereal bars (check the sugar content, it's usually over 25 percent with very little protein to balance this out), any crisps or other high carbohydrate foods.

Nuts and seeds seem almost too simple, but they are just perfect. Full of nutrients, easy to carry around with you, and widely available. You can add some fruit, like an apple or some berries – just don't make a daily habit of the very sweet ones like bananas, mangos or grapes. Check my website for suppliers of portable snacks you can buy in the shops: http://www.superwellness.co.uk/eat-well-at-work/recommended-suppliers/)

It's useful to keep a pack or two of nuts or seeds in your glove compartment or in your bag, something to fall back onto if you haven't had time to plan in advance.

If you stop en route for a break, then you could also pack a small pot of hummus (providing the protein) with some oatcakes or vegetable sticks, and you'd probably find this combination available in most motorway service stations now too.

HABIT 20: DANCING WITH STRESS
Every day, a quarter of a million people miss work because of stress, with 75 percent of all illnesses thought to be stress-related. And yet it is something which you can never eliminate. It's just part

of being alive! There will always be things that don't go your way, people with unrealistic expectations (including you!) and schedules that put you under pressure. Getting rid of stress itself is not going to happen, but we are not completely powerless. What we can do is improve our *resilience* to stress, learn to 'dance' with it so that it doesn't get in the way of living our life to its full potential, and in some cases maybe even works to our advantage.

The physical effects of stress
Make no mistake, stress is not just 'all in the mind' – there are very specific physical effects to it, as stress hormones programme your body for a specific type of situation, as in the times when our ancestors would have to recruit all of their best running skills to escape from a charging sabre tooth tiger – the famous 'fight or flight' reaction. The biological effects of this reaction are well known: we release stress hormones, mainly adrenaline, and cortisol, and their role is to mobilise resources to the fore functions which help save our life in that situation. In other words, things like increasing sugars in the bloodstream to fuel the brain and muscle cells, accelerating heartbeat, dilating pupils. However to do this, resources are diverted away from other functions, not deemed essential at that moment, like for example the digestive and immune functions. Your digestion won't suffer too much from an event like this happening once in a while, but if it is a permanent state, then it might cause it to underperform in a chronic way. Little wonder that stress is so often connected to conditions like irritable bowel syndrome, and a tendency to catch every bug circulating because the immune system is not functioning at its peak.

How we react to stress
New research is showing that it's the way we perceive stress that counts.

One study[30], which looked at almost 30,000 people, concluded that those who believed stress had a harmful impact on their health had a *43%* increased risk of death. At a similar level of stress, those who did not perceive its effects as negative were amongst the least likely to die. Another eye-opening study[31] came to a similar conclusion, advising us to view stress as helpful because it enables the body to recruit all of its resources. This perception is said to produce less damaging effects than the conventional view that stress is simply debilitating.

So what these studies seem to be saying is essentially: don't worry about the stress, just get on with it!

And yes, there are adrenaline junkies, and people who seem to thrive on stress, and possibly, in the light of the research mentioned above, this is indeed because it causes us to recruit all of our best resources in order to function in a more optimal way. And this can feel good.

However, even if you manage not to be paranoid about stress, that's not a reason to put your body under pressure unnecessarily. If you can avoid certain stressful situations, or improve your resilience so that fewer situations actually do stress you, then all the better.

Reducing stressful situations

It's easy to get caught up in a daily routine, without realising that perhaps it's time to question it. So it can be a useful exercise from time to time to take a step back and look at your schedule with a fresh pair of eyes. Stressful situations often bring to mind time pressure – worrying about fitting it all in. Are you taking on too much? I've been as guilty as anyone of wanting to cram my diary full of activities – courses, social gatherings, ambitious work goals, and all of the other life commitments. Especially when I started my business, SuperWellness. I felt frustrated that I wasn't getting where I wanted to be fast enough. My life was very full, and I thoroughly enjoyed all of these stimulating activities, but I was running myself ragged! Eventually I had to slow down and let a lot of this 'activity' fall by the wayside. Suddenly I wasn't driving or catching trains here there and everywhere, attending workshops and being involved in numerous projects – I just focused on a few priorities and began to feel I was finally making progress – what a relief! Are there ways you could gain from simplifying and focusing too?

Think of all the people and things that are causing you stress, and whether they are worth it, or whether there might be ways of reducing the burden. It might sound harsh, but it really is worth questioning some relationships and whether they are still really mutually beneficial. As Oprah Winfrey said: "Surround yourself with people who are going to lift you higher."

On a more mundane level, are there ways you could improve the logistics of your life? Are there things you are doing out of habit, which you could do differently? Could you delegate more? Do you need to make that five hour drive, or would a Skype call do the job?

Improving your resilience to stress with what you eat
The better shape your body and mind are in, the better equipped you'll be to cope with stress. Stress taxes your body in very specific ways, so nutrition does play a role in improving your coping mechanisms. Your adrenal glands (where stress hormones are produced) need a wide range of nutrients to function optimally, in particular vitamin C, so a nutrient dense diet with lots of fresh vegetables (and some fruit) is a good foundation.

Blood sugar balance plays a big part in our stress response too. When you experience a blood sugar crash, your adrenal glands will kick into action and release the stress hormone cortisol to compensate for your low blood glucose. Cortisol triggers a release of sugar from the body itself to allow you to keep going. So effectively, blood sugar lows trigger a stress response. So one of the most effective ways of countering stress through diet is by balancing your blood sugars (see chapter 2).

Strategies for changing your mind

Even with the most perfect diet in the world, you will never be able to completely counter the damage stress can cause. The main reason we experience stress is our negative reaction to events rather than the events themselves. So the key to improving your resilience to stress is working on how you handle situations. You don't have to be an expert in stress to know that when you feel tired, the normal events of the day feel more overwhelming, irritating and harder to cope with generally. So the first strategy will hardly come as a surprise:

Take a break!

- **Vary your activities:** breaks are scientifically proven to boost focus and productivity. The brain uses a lot of energy. The best way to recharge that energy is to step away from the screen and move to get the blood flowing. Even switching focus from one activity to the other can significantly improve your effectiveness[32] as your resources decline rapidly when you focus on a single task for a long period of time.

- **Take short breaks:** researcher Nathaniel Kleitman did some fascinating studies into 'ultradian rhythms', concluding that a 90 minute work period followed by a break seemed to be the ideal work to rest ratio[33].

- **Holidays:** don't forget the power of longer breaks. Holidays help you see the bigger picture, and studies have shown that your wellbeing is boosted by the anticipation for up to eight weeks beforehand[34].

Mindfulness and other techniques

There are techniques you can explore to improve your resilience to stress, and the practice of mindfulness is among the most studied, and successful. The Mental Health Foundation describes it as "a way of paying attention to the present moment, using techniques like meditation, breathing and yoga. It helps us become more aware of our thoughts and feelings so that instead of being overwhelmed by them, we're better able to manage them.

In other words, these techniques help you put more 'space' in your mind, so you can step back and observe your emotions instead of being ruled by them. From personal experience, it's important to be honest about the techniques that work best for you. I've met a lot of people who struggle with 'meditation'. Just the thought of sitting in silence for longer than five minutes is a stress in itself and in these cases, it's best to take a different approach to begin with – for instance doing something more physical that requires your mind to focus on and become aware of what your body is doing (like yoga). Whatever you are likely to stick to. Personally I always find yoga much easier to get into than mindfulness meditation, however convincingly someone is telling me how I *should* be meditating!

Bear in mind also that there are many different meditation techniques, from Zen to Transcendental, and numerous 'guided' apps. Finding and practising a technique over time will help focus your attention and concentration and give you more control over your emotions. Mindfulness has been proven to help with stress, by reducing your cortisol levels[35]. And it also has positive effects on anxiety, depression and addictive behaviours, as well as physical problems like hypertension, heart disease and chronic pain. But other techniques can be very effective as well.

If you feel that what's going on in your mind is holding you back, then think about how dearly this is costing you – your performance at work, your relationships with other people and your general happiness. Adopting a regular practice to work on your mind is good mental hygiene, and worth starting as quickly as possible.

Check out my website for links to meditation and mindfulness tools: http://www.superwellness.co.uk/eat-well-at-work/resources/.

HABIT 20: RELAXING AND CHEWING
This is a really important practical application of the previous habit: dancing with stress. Particularly in a work environment.

When we surveyed the employees we work with at SuperWellness, we found that around 80% of them on average take their lunch at their desk.

Scrolling through Facebook, or checking the latest BBC news whilst enjoying your sandwich (or low GL preparation!) might seem like a relaxing distraction and a good way to take some time out, but in fact physiologically, your body is still under stress.

Simply looking at a screen is a stressor for the brain as the flickering light and huge amounts of data overwhelm your normal processing capacity and put you into 'fight or flight' mode.

As we've seen in the previous habit, your nervous system directs all of your body's resources towards functions it considers necessary for dealing with an emergency situation (the sabre tooth tiger!) It diverts resources away from digestion, deemed not immediately necessary for survival. Gastric juices won't flow as they should, food won't be broken down sufficiently for you to get the maximum amount of nutrients from it. Food which has been poorly digested upstream may cause gas and bloating, because it starts to ferment and putrefy in the intestines (nice), disrupting the delicate balance of bacteria in the gut. Over time, this can have devastating effects on your digestive system, leading to symptoms which often get labelled 'irritable bowel syndrome' or IBS.

Unconscious eating
And it's not just the switch into 'fight or flight' mode which is undesirable, it's also the fact that our attention is being diverted away from what we are doing, leading to unconscious eating. This means we are not savouring our food, probably not chewing it sufficiently, and probably also eating much more than we really need to. Changing these habits will have hugely beneficial results.

'Rest and digest'
When your body is in 'rest and digest' mode, you'll benefit from optimal digestion and absorb maximum amounts of nutrients from your food. This means that your nervous system will be geared to 'pressing all the right buttons' for the complex digestive processes to take place.

How to switch into 'rest and digest'?

- Avoid looking at a screen while you are eating

- Move away from your desk and sit somewhere where you can be relaxed

- Chew each mouthful well - ideally until the food is almost liquefied to make sure it's coated with digestive enzymes

So it's been a busy week of travelling, staying in hotels, dancing with stress... time for some socialising now, and coming to terms with not being perfect! Let's begin week 4.

Chapter 6

Week 4: socialising & falling off the wagon

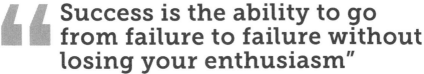

Success is the ability to go from failure to failure without losing your enthusiasm"
Sir Winston Churchill

HABIT 22: DEALING EFFECTIVELY WITH CRAVINGS

Cravings are so common that it would be easy to believe they are a normal part of life, just like feeling hungry is. And yet they are actually quite different from real hunger, they are not a necessary evil and don't have to be a serious hindrance to your everyday life, if you take the right steps to get rid of them. And it's well worth it! Think about it: this obsession with food – planning what to get, how to get it, when to get it, whether you should or should not, all the endless internal debates. And then the guilt, and the cycle starts again. How much of your internal dialogue are cravings occupying? How much energy are they sapping in your life?

Imagine how much more you could achieve each day, and over the years, if you could be free of cravings, able to concentrate for sustained periods of time, without the thought of food even crossing your mind.

Well you could just be a few days away from this freedom if you started doing the right things today. Because cravings are just the sign that something has gone out of balance and you can eliminate them with a diet that gives your body everything it needs. Ready?

What triggers food cravings?

Cravings go hand in hand with blood sugar imbalances, and this seems to work on two levels. The first level is simply the result of experiencing a dip in blood sugars: your cells - especially your brain cells - are suddenly starved of fuel and you can almost hear them screaming: 'give me some sugar! NOW!' Now the dip doesn't mean you need to be eating more sugar on a regular basis. Too much sugar or carbohydrate foods that release sugar very fast, raising your blood sugars fast too, and it's the dip that follows which causes the problem.

There is another level which glucose operates on to keep you stuck in the cycle of cravings: its addictive nature. Glucose has been shown to activate the brain's opioid system and trigger addiction in a similar way to nicotine or cocaine[36].

So number one suspect: sugar. There are other reasons as well, the first being that some foods – like chocolate - are involved in the release of endorphins, which give you a sense of relaxation. So if you're feeling stressed, it's no wonder you'll seek out those foods. You can also crave foods that contain nutrients you are lacking. For example chocolate contains high levels of iron (which can be depleted during the menstrual cycle) and magnesium (the 'relaxing mineral', very much in demand in stressful times).

What can you do about cravings?

Once a craving is there, it's often too late to do anything about it – it's a powerful physiological outcome that just seems to override any attempt by your rational brain at exercising willpower. It's a common pattern: you give into the craving, you feel guilty and beat yourself up. And then you have to go and buy a bar of chocolate to make yourself feel better. So the key really is in *preventing* cravings before they happen, and the good news is, there are proven ways you can do this. I see it working for people all the time.

The key is to provide your body and your brain with a steady supply of all the fuel and nutrients they need. Just the right dose of glucose, at the right pace, and generous measures of goodness in the food you eat. Think that every forkful is an opportunity to top up your levels of valuable minerals, vitamins, fats, proteins and natural plant compounds.

Actually, when you start to follow the habits I've covered in the earlier chapters, you'll notice that cravings are one of the first things to fade away. This will be a very good sign that you're on the right track.

Be prepared however that when you start to reduce sugar in your diet, your cravings might actually feel worse for a few days – it's worth getting through this, as life will be so much easier on the other side.

If you remember three things about preventing cravings in the early days, it's these:

- Always have tasty, protein rich snacks close to hand (a handful of almonds with a couple of squares of dark chocolate might just beat off the lure of the chocolate bar from the snack machine)

- Focus on building a good protein based breakfast into your daily routine – this will reduce cravings and hunger even late in the afternoon

- Remember that cravings have a physiological reason and you need to address them on that level – don't have unrealistic and self defeating expectations of willpower.

HABIT 23: DEALING WITH A BAD DAY

Ok, let's not pretend that making lifestyle changes is plain sailing all the way. Your head might be telling you one thing, and your emotions will be pulling you in other directions at times. All sorts of things will get in the way: well meaning colleagues offering you biscuits and munching chocolate just under your nose, boredom, tiredness, feeling like you need 'a treat' (and forgetting that the way you'll feel afterwards is far from a treat!), or just being in situations where you haven't got much choice – your Grandmother's made you a sticky toffee pudding which is about 80% sugar, and you don't want to hurt her feelings.

You might have bad days and you might have bad weeks, or even several weeks when other priorities seem to take over, and healthy habits fade into the background.

The thing is, this is likely to happen at some point, unless you are super-humanly disciplined and focused. So actually, it's much better to accept it, and expect it, so that when it does happen, it doesn't feel like a failure, but just part of the journey. You see, if you set your sights on perfection, then you set yourself up to fail, and eventually to give up altogether.

The more times you try to make changes and fail, the more disheartened you are likely to feel about the whole idea. Being discouraged by so-called failure is the one biggest mistake I've seen people make, and they scupper their future health because of it.

The advice I give, again and again to the people I work with is: "Do your best, and if you have a bad day, don't beat yourself up. Just get back on track again the following day."

In their brilliant book 'Changing for Good', psychology researchers James Prochaska and his colleagues described this phenomenon of 'relapse'. It's a normal occurrence, which happens somewhere along the six stages you go through for overcoming bad habits, and if you can move on from it, then you'll come out even stronger on the other side. They write: "People who take action and fail in the next month are twice as likely to succeed over the next six months than those who don't take any action at all."

The key is to get back on track. If you give up, then all your previous efforts will be wasted.

So how can you make sure you are equipped to deal with these 'relapses'?

- First, make sure you've got expectations that are not setting you up for failure: 80/20 is a good rule of thumb: be good

80 percent of the time, and accept that the remaining 20 percent will not be perfect.

- Learn from your relapses – be aware of how you feel the next day and you might want to consider what triggered this temporary sideways step (going away on holiday, certain emotions like anger or boredom, certain people).

- Get back on track with small goals you can achieve easily. A lot of people are tempted to go the other way with very harsh goals (almost like a punishment!) and end up making it even less appealing to stick with good intentions. If you set yourself ridiculously achievable goals then you're likely to go beyond and feel a really encouraging sense of achievement. For example, if you haven't been exercising for several weeks, then a goal to put a gym class in the diary is more likely to happen than suddenly planning to visit the gym five times in a week.

If you've let the good habits slip for a few weeks or more, then you might want to go back to basics, making sure you're planning your meals, shopping and exercise and being strict with your snacks for a while.

I've often come across people I'd worked with years previously, and they had the feeling that they had let all of their good habits slip – actually when we talked through their daily routine, all the key habits were still in place and if they did a body composition test, they were often surprised at how good the results were. Never underestimate the power of every small habit change you make!

HABIT 24: GOING OUT FOR DRINKS AND MAKING THE BEST CHOICES

Socialising is part and parcel of working life, and one of the biggest fears I've heard people mention when they've started a nutrition programme with me, is that I might expect them to behave in a way that alienates colleagues and turns them into a social pariah!

Just to put your mind at rest, this doesn't have to be the case – the goal is to help you perform better and achieve more, certainly not to put you at a disadvantage because you don't fit in.

Let's face it, drinking is one of the pillars of social life in most organisations in the UK. You might be lucky enough to be part of an organisation where you won't be judged negatively for not drinking, and maybe even supported towards this, but in reality, there are still many workplaces where drinking is part of the culture and moving towards healthier habits can involve a delicate balancing act.

So what are some of the best courses of action my clients have taken?

One of my clients, Gary, found that his colleagues had no problem respecting temporary alcohol detoxes. 'I'm not drinking this month' was a great way of getting off the hook, and still being in the in-crowd, no questions asked. Similarly, you can set other clear boundaries, like 'I'm not drinking during the week', and colleagues might feel that these temporary breaks are less of a 'threat' to the culture of bonding around alcohol.

I'm not saying you should give up alcohol completely necessarily – it's up to you to set yourself the aims that feel right for you. Chances are, if you go out for regular office drinks, or outside of work socially, you probably enjoy the first glass or two and anything after that is just 'because it's there' and because everyone else is drinking too. I found myself (probably as I got older and less resilient!) that those drinks you're not enjoying come at such a high price the next day, when the hangover strikes, that they were simply not worth it. Just being more aware of this can help change these behaviours, encouraging you to drink more slowly, or to replace every other drink with water.

So we've looked at some of the behaviours around alcohol, but how exactly does it affect you, and how can it fit into a healthy lifestyle?

One of the major issues with alcohol is – you've guessed it! – how it affects your blood sugars. Not all alcoholic drinks raise your blood sugars – spirits on their own don't at all in fact. It's the mixers that come with them which do. Beers, lagers, wines, sherry and liqueurs all play havoc with your blood sugars as soon as you've had more than one or two units. One thing a lot of people notice is that when they've had a few drinks, they find themselves awake in the middle of the night and unable to fall back to sleep. This is because although alcohol initially raises your blood sugars, it also inhibits your liver from releasing glucose (which it tends to do during the night to keep your blood sugars level as you're effectively fasting for quite a number of hours). So what you experience then is mild hypoglycaemia (a drop in blood sugars). This is why you'll most probably be craving a high carbohydrate breakfast the next morning!

Apart from disrupting your metabolism (and remember, when that happens, and you start getting blood sugar highs and lows, and releasing more insulin, you begin to store more fat, and struggle with dips in energy and concentration), excessive alcohol also comes with the heavy price tag of a hangover!

If time is money, then a hangover really is pretty expensive (and avoidable!) Think of the cost to you of a day - or more, as you get older- of varying degrees of headache, dizziness, confusion, tiredness, and if things are really bad, actual sickness... you've got to ask – as I did at one stage: was it really worth it?

And talking about the 'cost' to you in terms of performance, there is a longer term price to pay for regular excessive consumption too. Unfortunately, your brain – this precious long-term asset of yours - is not coming out unscathed either.

How does alcohol affect your brain?
The reason people enjoy alcohol is also the reason why it's so dangerous for your brain. It's able to cross straight through the blood brain barrier, which is normally there to protect your valuable brain cells, and come into direct contact with them.

You've probably heard that alcohol is a depressant, and this is because it alters your brain chemistry. It does this by suppressing certain neurotransmitters (brain chemicals), like glutamate, which are normally in charge of increasing brain activity and energy levels. So effectively, it slows you down – hence the slurred speech, delayed reaction and foggy memory.

Sure, you'll feel good initially because alcohol also triggers a release of dopamine, the 'feel good chemical'. The problem is that, if you start to rely regularly on alcohol to feel better or to relax, you'll no longer feel those effects, but the reward centres in your brain will certainly be hooked. And so will you.

Far outweighing the short-term gratification of dopamine, is the longer term effect that regular drinking has on serotonin – another so called 'feel good' chemical – which it suppresses, leading to lower mood, depression and anxiety.

So not really a recipe for success, and I should also add that drinking regularly for a long period of time causes permanent damage to the memory system. Remembering new information can become harder, so learning new things can take longer. Not to mention that alcohol also reduces your higher-level thinking, in other words your ability to think in abstract terms.

Is alcohol always bad?
Having outlined all the ways in which excessive alcohol can put a spanner in the works, you will of course have no doubt come across all the reports in the press of the positive effects that alcohol, especially red wine, can have *in moderation*. Moderation is of course the key word here, and what it means is essentially no more than a glass of wine for women and maybe two for men.

> The NHS guidelines are three to four units of alcohol a day maximum for men and not more than two to three units a day for women. One unit equals 10ml or 8g of pure alcohol. A 250ml (large) glass of 12% red wine has about three units of alcohol. A 175ml (medium) glass has about two units.

Some studies have reported that moderate alcohol can reduce the risk of depression[37] and that resveratrol, a compound found in (mainly red) grape skins can help reduce the risk of dementia and certain cancers.

Having said this, I wouldn't recommend starting to drink for health purposes if you don't drink currently – it's not worth embarking on such a slippery slope!

So what are the key takeaways on alcohol?

- If you feel that you're relying on alcohol regularly as a way to unwind, and you're having more than the recommended number of units, then this is most probably a habit worth working on. Taking an alcohol free month is a good way to undo some of its addictive effects, and give your health a good all-round boost. In fact it's probably one of the most effective things you can do for yourself in a short space of time.

- Take regular alcohol free days to avoid building up a tolerance, and also focus on the enjoyment you get. Start to notice when you've passed the enjoyment stage (and are entering the hangover zone) – are you just drinking out of habit or to be social?

- The challenge in reducing alcohol is often: "What on earth to have instead?" especially when you go to pubs and bars. Here are a few suggestions for minimising the impact of alcohol or choosing alternatives that are not packed with sugar:

  - o Mixers that won't affect your blood sugars so much: plain soda with a slice of lime rather than lime syrup, tomato juice – Bloody Mary anyone?
  - o White wine spritzer – sip slowly!
  - o A glass of red wine (slightly less blood sugar impact and more health benefits than white)

    o   Soda or sparkling water with a slice of lime or lemon
    o   Cranberry juice mixed with lots of soda water
    o   Tomato juice (Virgin Mary)

HABIT 25: HANDLING PEER PRESSURE

When I ask the clients I coach what they struggle with most in trying to establish healthier habits, it's very often that they reply: "other people!"

Food and drink are real bonding agents. When you think about it, there are so many 'traditions' within families or between friends or colleagues. If you suddenly start turning down the Birthday cake that's going around the office, you might find this doesn't go down too well with everyone. Some people might feel threatened when they see you suddenly seeming to distance yourself from these 'rituals', especially when it comes to drinking alcohol.

And it's the same outside of work too – how do you deal with: "Oh go on! One more won't do you any harm"? And do you crack under the pressure of "Well you're not much fun to be around"?

When you begin to make changes, be prepared for people to try to talk you out of it or steer you off track, intentionally or not. Other people might not understand what you are trying to do. I worked with a client called Amanthi, whose mother lived at home with the family, and cooked all of their evening meals. Her mother had good intentions when she prepared comforting Sri Lankan food with copious fluffy white rice – it was her way of showing her affection for the family, and Amanthi had to tread delicately so as not to hurt her feelings. Eventually she managed to persuade her Mother to cook brown rice instead and Amanthi made herself a large salad to accompany a smaller portion of the delicious meal that had been prepared for her.

Hopefully you will have lots of peers encouraging and supporting you too, but handling 'peer pressure' is something you will need a strategy for. You'll need to form a new habit around how you respond to this pressure from other people, and like any new habit, it takes a deliberate intention and lots of practice before it becomes 'second nature'.

Here are some of these 'strategies' which my clients have used and found to be effective:

- Considering what the intentions are, driving that person to put pressure on you: one of my clients, Peter, had a neighbour who he often socialised with down the pub – he would usually end up drinking far more than he really wanted to, and regret it the next day. Looking back on their drinking relationship in the cold light of day made him realise that his neighbour was actually using Peter as an excuse to be able to go out and drink heavily. If he was with a friendly neighbour then somehow, it seemed more acceptable to his family for him to regularly stagger back home. I remember Peter saying to me: 'I actually feel *used*!' Realising this made it much easier for Peter to assert his own choices without feeling bad.

- Accepting that in some situations, it's okay to compromise. If your great Aunt who you visit once a year, has prepared a banoffee pie for dessert, because you once told her that was your favourite, then maybe it's not worth hurting her feelings by turning it down. Keep the 80/20 rule in mind, and just put it down to the 20% of times when it's ok to go off track a bit.

- Practising saying 'No' comfortably. There's definitely an art to this – it generally involves a big warm smile and lots of eye contact (so the person won't feel rejected) and a confident, assertive 'No thank you'. You might even find you don't need to explain why (do you really want to give the other person an opportunity to explain why, actually, in their eyes, your excuse isn't valid?). If you feel you do need an excuse, then keep it as vague as possible: 'I'm cutting out sugar at the moment' is hard to argue with!

- If you're feeling confident, then why not put on a bit of peer pressure of your own? In a good way. Most people are receptive to advice that will make them feel better. If you can explain to someone why they feel rubbish an hour after an energy drink, and pass around some of your healthy snacks for them to try, you might well make some converts. On the other hand, if you sense that your advice is not welcome, do back off! Becoming a health evangelist (whether the audience is receptive or not) is a common mistake people make when they start discovering how much difference nutrition can make – me included! It can be hard to accept that not everyone is quite ready for that message yet.

HABIT 26: CHOOSING WELL WHEN EATING OUT

When I ask my clients about their week ahead and what might scupper their plans for keeping on track, they often mention meals out. In fact, eating out doesn't have to be unhealthy. It's usually easy to find good nutritious food in most restaurants nowadays, or to ask for some slight changes that will make your meal perfect.

Preparation is key

One thing I would recommend, if you can, is to check the menu in advance. Especially if you are staying away for a couple of days or more, do a search on local restaurants, and check their menus. When you are tired after a long drive, or a day with clients, making a decision on what to eat can be hard work, let alone resisting the temptation of less healthy options.

Keep your balanced plate in mind, and it usually becomes easy to find an Italian or French meal with meat or fish - having steered clear of the pizza and pasta section of the menu! Remember there's nothing to stop you asking the waiter for some slight modifications: fewer potatoes, more green vegetable sides, requesting olive oil and lemon (or balsamic vinegar) instead of sugar laden dressings, or asking them in advance not to bring bread to the table.

With Indian, Thai or Chinese food, respect the same balance, choose protein rich mains with very little white rice or bread. It requires rethinking what you've been used to, simply out of habit, but is no less tasty... and much more satisfying.

What can you choose? Here are some typical menu options that should please your taste buds at lesser cost to your body:

Italian: choose: Fish or meat with vegetables Large salad with protein (parma ham, chicken, mozzarella) Mussels	Avoid/limit: Pasta Bruschetta Dough balls Pizza Deep fried calamari
Indian: choose: Dhal and chickpea dishes, Tandoori dishes Chicken tikka Yoghurt Most curries	Avoid/limit: Rice and bread Poppadoms Mango or other pickles (tend to be high in sugar)
Thai / Chinese: choose: Stir fries with protein Tom Yum soup Satay skewers Curries with coconut milk Tofu	Avoid/limit: Deep fried food Share a portion of noodles or rice with someone Prawn crackers Noodle soup
Pub: choose: Stews Roast with lots of vegetables All day breakfast (bacon, sausage, eggs, tomato, mushrooms)	Avoid/limit: Replace mash, chips, pasta with veg or salad Burgers (remove half the bun)

MENU SUSSED

HEALTHY
SNACKS

So having navigated the perils of socialising, peer pressure, and simply being a less than perfect human being (*sigh*), now let's look at some things you can do to take your healthy habits to a whole new level. Let's begin week 5!

Chapter 7

Week 5: My body is a temple

 **For every disciplined effort there is a multiple reward"**
Anthony Robbins

27. Trying new recipes at home
28. Batch cooking
29. Detoxing (from time to time)
30. Getting your power sleep
31. Reading food labels

HABIT 27: TRYING NEW RECIPES AT HOME

If you want to stick to a healthy programme long term, and not just for a couple of months, then it's going to be important to keep things interesting. Everyone needs some change on the menu, otherwise boredom will lead you to drift back into old favourites, and you'll barely notice it's happening.

So trying new recipes is an important habit to get into. Without it becoming an obsession or taking over your evenings and weekends (unless that's what you want!)

New recipes don't have to be complicated or require much preparation. If anything, it's the really easy, quick and tasty recipes you want to be on the lookout for. Maybe thinking about it in terms of 'food ideas' is less daunting than 'recipes'. Being a vegetarian myself, with an intolerance to gluten, you can imagine how much this narrows the field. I'm constantly scouting for new and interesting meals, and I'm amazed at the endless discoveries I make. We are brought up with certain traditions around food, particularly as far as gluten is concerned. A few years ago, I couldn't even have imagined surviving on a diet with no bread or flour in it. It's been a real eye opener experimenting with cakes that require no flour, and garlic bread made with ground almonds – delicious!

Most people have a repertoire of recipes they rotate on a regular basis. We have our favourites at home, and some of these tend to drift off the menu and lose their appeal. Sometimes you can feel 'stuck in a rut' with nothing that really seems to hit the spot. So the hunt for a new favourite begins.

One tip for you is to cook in what I call a 'modular' way. I do this all the time at home, and all I mean by this is the idea of varying the ingredients you use in a single recipe. So for example, if you regularly make the pasta recipe in the recipe section at the end of this book, with Halloumi, you can vary the protein, so you can use hot smoked salmon instead of Halloumi, or grilled chicken. Vary the vegetables, so you might use avocado instead of sugar snap peas. You can even switch the pasta for brown rice, or quinoa. Visit the resources page on my website to download my 'Modular recipe system' along with other food ideas – including ready to eat meals you can buy: http://www. superwellness.co.uk/eat-well-at-work/resources/

It's always a good idea to have a couple of good nutritionally sound recipe books at hand, to browse through, and perhaps try a couple of new things each month. Subscribing to a few nutritionally oriented recipe blogs is a good idea too. Again I list a few of my favourites in the resources section of my site: http://www.superwellness.co.uk/eat-well-at-work/resources/

I also regularly publish the recipes I come up with on my blog, so for a regular influx of new ideas, don't hesitate to subscribe at http://www.superwellness.co.uk/blog/.

HABIT 28: BATCH COOKING

This is a good habit to get into if you want to eat a maximum amount of home cooked food for a minimal investment in effort and time!

You can batch cook most things, and enjoy the fruits of this during your busy week. Here are a few ideas:

- Hard-boiled eggs: cook six in one go and that's your breakfast, snack or lunch protein sorted for three days. Hard-boiled eggs will keep in the fridge for up to a week with their shells on, a couple of days less if peeled.

- Rice or quinoa: cook a big batch and freeze small portions in freezer bags. Ideal for salads, or to go with a quick stir-fry in the evening.

- It goes without saying, stews, soups and curries are perfect candidates for batch cooking. Even better if you have a slow cooker (which can do all the cooking while you're at work). This way of cooking, at a low temperature, preserves a lot more of the nutrients in your food than other methods. All that's required is planning so you have the ingredients at the ready.

- Any plastic containers you still have available from takeaway days can come in handy, so you can store you own private stock of home-made takeaways. When I suggested this recently at a company I was working at, a couple of people looked at me in amazement that I would have a stash of takeaway containers at home. 'So you have takeaways?!' Nobody's perfect, and anyway, takeaways are not always bad!

- Oat pancakes (see the recipe section at the end of this book). Several of my clients have got into the habit of making a large batch of these at the weekend, freezing them and then just popping them in the toaster on week mornings.

- Porridge or bircher muesli: oats are better soaked overnight (because this breaks down the phytic acid, a natural chemical that blocks the absorption of many vitamins and minerals) so if you really wanted hassle-free mornings, you could prepare two or three bowls in advance, and just heat them up in the morning. Otherwise the uncooked version, to which you can add nuts and seeds is the Swiss classic, bircher muesli.

- A large bowl of quinoa or rice salad will stand you in good stead for a couple of lunches (don't keep rice in the fridge for longer than two days though).

- Roasted chicken wings – why just do enough for dinner? You could eat them as snacks the next couple of days too.

Whatever you cook, always ask yourself whether you could cook more of it, and save yourself time the next day. You'll be amazed at how much time you can save by approaching food preparation in this way.

HABIT 29: DETOXING (FROM TIME TO TIME)

Doing a detox in Thailand was the turning point that made me realise the power of nutrition and eventually led me to change career paths. Whilst real long-term change requires a less dramatic approach, changing habits one by one, doing a 'detox' could be one of the most life changing things you ever undertake.

So what does 'detox' mean exactly?

Effectively, it's a way of giving your body a break, particularly your liver. Your liver is charged with the heavy burden of dealing with the constant influx of toxins – harmful chemical compounds – from the outside world as well as those your body creates itself. It has the very important function of breaking down this toxic waste to render it less harmful, and then assisting in its safe removal from the body.

Some cynics say that 'detoxing' is useless because the liver is made to do this job anyway. In fact, the toxic load we subject our livers to now is much higher than it's ever been, with countless harmful chemicals coming in through the food chain, as well as through our skin (yes our skin absorbs all the chemicals that are used in creams and shampoos, and they then travel via our bloodstream to be dealt with by the liver). Just the way you feel after a detox is enough to tell you that it's been effective!

You can do a detox on any level you choose. Obviously the stricter you go, the more challenging it will be, and the more rewarding as well. When I did my first detox in Thailand, it was a seven day fast, and I felt very ill for most of it! This is why it's important if you are doing quite an extreme form of detox, to do it in supervised conditions.

Otherwise, there are milder forms of detox you can undertake, and certainly if you want to give yourself a boost, with something that's manageable from home, then this is what I would recommend. It's what I call the essential detox, and you can extend it with further aspects if you choose to. You can do the essential detox for any length of time you choose, but for any meaningful results, seven days is really a minimum.

When is the best time for a detox?
You can do a detox at any time that's convenient for you, however I would just make the following recommendations:

- Never start a detox if you know you're going into a really busy time (you will feel tired at times, especially in the beginning, and you might struggle to stick with it)

- Weekends are a good time to start, as you can get organised and get over the worst of any withdrawal symptoms

- You might want to make sure that you will be able to get plenty of sleep in the first week. It's during sleep that much of the detox work will be done – just as you wouldn't expect to carry on working on your laptop while running a 'disk clean-up programme' on it.

- January is always a good time, as you'll probably be in good company. Psychologically, it's good to start the New Year with a boost to the system!

- Detoxes are generally easier in the spring or when the weather is warmer. Large salads and vegetable juices are not so appealing when it's cold outside.

Essential detox guidelines:

Sticking to the healthy habits described so far, plus:
No alcohol
No coffee or caffeinated drinks
Completely avoid food containing additives, colourings or other toxic chemicals (washing fruit and vegetables very thoroughly or buying organic)
8 portions of fruit and veg a day (at least 6 being veg)
High protein breakfast at least 5 days a week (protein shake or eggs / fish)
3 resistance exercise sessions in 7 days (swimming, weights, yoga, pilates, etc..) Or At least 20 minutes gentle exercise a day
2 litres of water a day
Oily fish 3x a week (or use flaxseed oil on salads)
Sleep – get to bed 1 hour earlier, get at least 7 hours
Avoid wheat (bread, pasta) – substitute with oatcakes, beans and lentils, oats, rice.
Avoid dairy (cow's milk, cheese, yogurt) – replace with goat's or sheep's cheese, yogurt and other milk substitutes (almond milk, coconut milk)

This is a good foundation for a detox, as you are eliminating foods and chemicals that burden your liver and your immune system, but at the same time providing a wealth of nutrients which your body needs to process your existing toxic load and repair itself.

Fasting

Fasting is a fascinating and controversial topic in nutrition. Recent research has shown how beneficial it can be. When it comes to fasting, there are also several options available, from cutting out everything bar water (definitely the hardest, and one I haven't attempted myself!) to so-called fasts that involve juicing.

The fast I did in Thailand (and have completed several times since then) does still involve ingesting various liquids. For a 'die hard' faster, it might seem like cheating because you do take a 'shake' every few hours, which contains psyllium husk (a fibre which helps cleanse your digestive tract), bentonite clay (a very fine clay – yes indeed! – which binds with toxins in the intestines and helps move them out) and can help yourself freely to a very light alkaline broth (made with various vegetables so that you get to absorb their vitamins and minerals). The psyllium expands in water, to make a very glutinous, jelly like shake indeed, so that you never really feel hungry as such. It is still challenging, as you miss food, chewing it and especially tasting it. You can feel exhausted at times, and even quite ill, as your body dredges up stored toxins. However these effects become much less dramatic, the second time around. In fact, as you become used to this regime (I try to do a similar fast once a year or every two years if I can) you can experience incredible energy while doing it. The type of energy that makes you feel unstoppable, and incredibly creative. This is how I also felt for a number of weeks after having completed the fast – and why I became so fascinated by nutrition!

So back to our 'Essential detox', which is more manageable in an everyday context. There are ways you can build on it, by helping the body get rid of even more toxic load during that time, and increase its effectiveness further.

Here are a few suggestions:
- Switching to **body care products** that don't contain harmful chemicals (the main harmful ingredients are sodium lauryl sulphate and parabens) – I've listed some of my favourite brands on my recommended supplier page: http://www.superwellness.co.uk/eat-well-at-work/recommended-suppliers/

- **Sauna and infra-red sauna sessions**: as you sweat, you excrete toxins through the skin. Infra-red saunas have been shown to be particularly effective for heavy metals[38], which are notoriously difficult to remove. A course of infra-red sauna sessions would be a very beneficial adjunct to giving up smoking, ridding yourself of heavy metals introduced into the body by cigarettes, such as cadmium and arsenic.

- **Massage:** a good therapist will free up toxins from your soft tissues and allow them to drain away via the lymphatic system (part of the circulation which carries waste products away from the tissues).

- **Vegetable juices:** not all juicing will have a beneficial long-term effect, even if you make all the juices yourself. Juices with too many fruit (essentially more than you could eat if you were eating the fruit whole) will burden your body with fructose, a type of sugar, which the liver converts directly into fat (most of which will immediately be deposited in the liver itself). With the right ingredients however, juicing can act almost like an intravenous infusion of readily absorbed nutrients and antioxidants to help the body repair and detoxify.

- **Add Epsom salts to your bath water:** as you detox, you might experience various aches and pains, not to mention fatigue, so a comforting hot bath can be ideal. Epsom salts contain Magnesium Sulfate which helps to draw toxins out through the skin. Make sure you only spend 15 minutes in the bath, as your skin will begin to reabsorb them after that!

So what's the take-home message?

A detox in the right context can be extremely effective, but don't expect it to be the answer to everything. If you do a detox expecting to lose weight and be healthy ever after, then these results are unlikely to last beyond a month if you're lucky, unless you keep going with your healthy habits in the background.

I recommend undertaking a detox to kick-start your wellness programme, or give yourself a well needed boost if you feel you've started to go off-track, or become demotivated. Whenever I become too reliant on caffeine (even with just one coffee a day) I know that a detox will be a good way to break that habit and 'reboot' my health.

What a detox does very effectively, and the reason why I recommend it to you, is that it gives you a taste for an optimum state of health. It helps you realise what you really should be aspiring to in daily life. Just functioning is not good enough – it's that unstoppable energy we should all be aiming for.

HABIT 30: GETTING YOUR POWER SLEEP

If you did nothing else but prioritise three of the 31 habits we cover in this book, then sleep would be among them. Getting good sleep is one of those areas in which very few people actually tick the box, and yet the benefits if they did, would be far reaching.

Sleep is undervalued, disdained, and sometimes downright frowned upon in our culture. Indulging our need to sleep is almost seen as a sign of weakness! The business world is full of stories of chief executives who start their working day at 5.00am and investment bankers who work through the night - sometimes with tragic consequences.

So why is this such a mistake?

If at first sight, sleep seems like nothing more than unproductive downtime, it is in fact essential maintenance and repair time for your body and brain. You've seen the state of buildings from the 60's which have been neglected... everything starts to peel away, decay and go wrong!

In fact to continue the analogy of sleep as essential maintenance, you can think of sleep as providing all important electrical power and keeping your wiring in good condition by recharging your nerve energy. Just as you would empty the big wheelie bins regularly and clean the stairwell, you need sleep to allow the body to detoxify. The walls and roof sometimes need care and attention in order to protect the inside of the building, and similarly good quality sleep is essential to keeping your immune system strong. And what about the wear and tear of daily comings and goings on floors? They sometimes need a fresh new covering just as your body needs time and energy to undo the ravages of stress. And let's not forget your home office, that place where you sometimes take some time out to file away bank statements, council tax bills and the cat's vaccination record... yes that's right, your memory needs a chance to do its filing too, and sleep helps to consolidate those neural connections.

Circadian rhythm

You may have heard about a study[39] which grabbed all the headlines when it was published, because it was so relevant to our times: scientists at Northwestern University in Chicago found that being exposed to the blue light from smartphones and computers in the evening disrupts our circadian rhythm. What does this mean? increased hunger levels, poor sleep and higher levels of insulin resistance[40] (in other words our cells are less able to use the glucose in our blood to produce energy – it can be the start of the slippery slope to diabetes type 2[41]).

So why is the circadian rhythm so important?

All of the hormones which regulate our metabolism are orchestrated around a 24 hour cycle based on the perception of light by our retina.

Because humans (unlike most other mammals) sleep in a single period of seven to nine hours, we need to maintain our glucose balance in spite of a long period of fasting during the night[42]. This is why our physiology works very differently depending on whether we're in the wake state or the sleep state. And the reason why we are so susceptible to disturbances in our rhythm, such as jet lag, shift work, or blue light in the evening. It's hardly surprising therefore that epidemiological studies consistently show an increased risk for type 2 diabetes for shift workers for instance.

Sleep, hormones and food

Have you ever noticed that you can't stop eating after a bad night's sleep? That's because poor sleep disrupts the hormones that regulate our appetite:

- It reduces leptin, which makes you feel full and satisfied

- It increases ghrelin, which you can blame for making you feel hungry even when your body has enough food (yes it's not just your imagination!)

- It decreases the chemicals serotonin and dopamine, making you crave sugary foods

And it's not just how you feel about food that's being affected by poor sleep, it's what your body does with it too:

- It decreases growth hormone, making it harder to burn fat and lay down lean muscle.

- It can directly affect the way our body handles glucose (whether it gets used as energy or stored as fat). Just one night of partial sleep restriction is enough to blunt our cells' insulin sensitivity the following day.

- And finally it increases cortisol, "the stress hormone", leading to the breakdown of muscle, increasing blood sugar and insulin (hence deposition of fat, mainly around your waist.)

How to use the power of sleep to your advantage
Research shows that we mostly need at least seven hours of good quality sleep, so what steps can you take if you haven't quite cracked it yet?

Timing and preparation

- Aim to get to bed around the same time each night, ideally around 10.00pm (or if that's a bit of leap, start by bringing bedtime forward by half an hour)

- Design your bedroom primarily to support good sleep. Keep it clean and uncluttered

- Listen to white noise or relaxation CDs

- Make sure you are exercising regularly

Eating and drinking

- Avoid snacking on sweet or starchy foods just before bedtime as they raise your blood sugar and inhibit sleep (or wake you up when your blood sugars drop!)

- For the same reason avoid or limit alcohol (ever woken up in the middle of the night after a few glasses too many?)

- If you do snack before bedtime, choose protein. It won't disturb your blood sugars as much and will provide L-tryptophan, a precursor to melatonin and serotonin

- Avoid caffeine as much as possible

Lighting:

- Avoid screens (TV, smartphones and computers) for at least an hour before the time you'd like to sleep

- Keep the lights down in the evening and don't turn them on if you have to get up during the night as bright light will affect your circadian rhythm.

HABIT 31: READING FOOD LABELS

Few people bother to decipher the small print on the back of the packet, and yet this simple action is enough to put you in control as an informed consumer. Whether you're choosing your lunch or doing your weekly shopping, reading the labels on what you buy is quite an eye opener and can certainly protect you from the risk of ever being fair game for the food advertisers again!

People are often quite shocked when I present photos of the food packaging they are familiar with, and then show them how to make sense of the nutrition information. Pictures of freshly ploughed fields, wholesome families, lean and athletic figureheads... all create an instant perception – but is it in line with reality?

Nutritional information

Reading the food labels might seem confusing at first, but when you know what to look for, it only takes a glance. Begin by looking at the 'nutritional information'. This lists calories and all the main categories of nutrients: protein, carbohydrates (of which sugars), fats (of which saturates), fibre and sodium. Most people look at the calorie content and maybe the amount of saturated fat. Calories, as I've mentioned before, have limited significance by themselves, and yet so many people wrongly perceive 'low calorie' to be synonymous with 'healthy'. Saturates are useful to look at, but as we now know, they are not the biggest threat to health. The most telling information to look for is the sugar percentage. This should be ten percent maximum for a 'sweet' food (you might be surprised at how many so called savoury foods contain more than this). Any more and no, it's certainly not a 'healthy' food.

Ingredients

Next, check the ingredients list. They are listed in order of weight, with the highest amounts first. Look for sugar and other sweeteners - often hidden because their names sound less familiar: glucose syrup, fructose syrup, corn syrup, fructose, honey, dextrose, maltodextrin, and many more. Often several appear in the same list. Look out for artificial ingredients too, colourings and chemical sweeteners. Sweeteners are supposed to save you the ill effects of sugar but increasing evidence is showing just how toxic some of them can be[43].

A good rule of thumb is: if you can't pronounce it, then it probably shouldn't be in your food!

Conclusion

> **"It is inspiring to realize that in choosing our response to circumstance, we powerfully affect our circumstance. When we change one part of the chemical formula, we change the nature of the results."**
> Stephen R. Covey

So here we are. We've reached the final part of this book, and I'm hoping that the 31 habits we've covered will provide you with a helpful structure to advance forward on your journey to ever greater wellness, energy and success.

This is not about a miracle one-month transformation – one habit a day, mastered. Bang. Habits take time to change, and yes, doing so when your schedule is packed and your mind seems even more full can be a delicate balancing act. All I will say is: don't underestimate the power of small, gradual, achievable steps.

Jeff Olson, author of 'The Slight Edge', one of my favourite books about changing habits, wrote that "the things you do every single day, the things that don't look dramatic, that don't even look like they matter, do matter. They not only make a difference—they make all the difference."

He also acknowledged this: "Here's the problem: every action that is easy to do, is also easy not to do." Filling a jug of water to place on your desk first thing in the morning is surely one of the easiest things to do. It's also very easy not to bother, to put it off to another day. If you are tempted *not to do* something that would be easy to do, it's worth remembering this: "The price of neglect is much worse than the price of the discipline."

Imagine what the price of neglect would be to you, one year, five years, ten years from now. What could it cost you, in terms of your health, your professional achievements and your general level of happiness?

So just keep showing up: one mouthful at a time, you can create higher energy, better health and optimum performance – all the way to the top!

About the Author

Angela Steel, the 'Healthy Habit Engineer', is a Naturopathic Nutritional Therapist by training. She specialises in nutrition-centred employee wellness, empowering people to optimise their potential by making well-informed adjustments to their diet and lifestyle.

Drawing on her previous life experience as a senior manager in the IT industry for many years, combined with a love of tasty food, Angela takes a down to earth approach to healthy eating.

Her workplace nutrition programme, the SuperWellness nutrition challenge has resulted in outstanding measurable benefits and enthusiastic feedback from employees and employers alike.

Angela is a Registered Naturopathic practitioner with the Complementary and Natural Healthcare Council (CNHC). She is also a core member of the Academy of Nutritional Medicine (AONM), which promotes clinical collaboration between Nutritional Therapists and Medical Doctors.

www.superwellness.co.uk

EMPOWER YOUR PEOPLE TO TAP INTO THEIR FULL POTENTIAL BY ENGAGING IN HEALTHY LIFESTYLE CHANGE

SUPER WELLNESS

Are you an employer, Human Resources Director, Rewards and Benefits Manager or occupational health professional? We can help you optimise your team's performance using nutrition. Imagine the difference you could make!

PROVEN SUCCESS

We've worked with organisations across all sectors, with consistently excellent feedback and results, helping them achieve:

- Improved employee wellness
- Revived team spirit & engagement
- Higher productivity and performance
- Enhanced CSR and reputation
- Reduced absenteeism
- Raised motivation

"For us, running a great business starts with healthy and happy employees. I'm delighted that Kuoni joined the SuperWellness challenge, a pioneering new concept in employee wellness which has had really meaningful results. The positive outcomes have been way beyond improved wellness, enhancing team spirit and motivation." **Derek Jones, Managing Director Kuoni**

"The interest has been phenomenal, the nutrition challenge has been the most talked about benefits initiative we've introduced this year. It's definitely something we are planning to run again next year." **Emma Cutbill, Benefits Manager at Incisive Media**

HOW WE CAN HELP YOU TOO
- **Measurable results** – we track and report on the success of our programmes
- **Engaging content** – captivating seminars by subject matter experts, explaining the 'why' with scientifically backed information
- Programmes geared for **practical implementation**, and a journey that's already been mapped out to ensure maximum success
- Team building wellness workshops that harness gamification to create **buzz and motivation**
- Presenters hand-picked and trained to our **high standard**

The result? More productive, engaged and motivated employees.

COMMENTS FROM PREVIOUS PARTICIPANTS:
"The 3 month challenge exceeded my expectations in every way! I would never want to go back to my old diet."NB

"Brilliant! Really interesting and easy to follow." GG

"I feel so much better in myself and the fact I've had little or no joint pain has been remarkable. I would definitely recommend this. Dawn Butcher

"It's been enjoyable and educational." KS

"A brilliant programme that benefits you at work as well as in your personal life." Nancy Verboom

"It's been motivating to do it together and great to share recipes and ideas." RN

"This has been a real eye opener. I've learned a lot, feel a lot better – it's been really helpful." Heidi Halling

"The format has been perfect and sessions were just the right length of time." JA

SOME OF OUR NUTRITION WORKSHOPS

The 7 Nutrition Habits of Highly Effective People	An inspiring introduction to nutrition for busy professionals. Lots of fascinating science based facts, and practical steps to make change happen.
Lose Weight and Gain Energy	Why do some people seem to struggle with their metabolism no matter what they do? We take a look at the 7 blocks to weight loss, encouraging people to take into account the connection between health and weight.
10 Steps to a Healthy Digestion	Digestive problems affect many people's lives, sometimes causing immense distress. We share: • The 3 top causes of digestive problems, • Why the gut is also known as 'the second brain' • Practical tips you can apply straight away, along with recipe ideas for gut friendly meals.
Food for the Brain – Nutrition Secrets for Boosting Stress Resilience and Brain Power	From poor concentration to anxiety and depression, it can seem to many that their brain is letting them down on a daily basis. How can we feed our brain so it serves us to the best of its capacity? We explain what the brain is made of, we reveal the 4 mind melters to avoid and the 5 brain foods that will boost performance. We end with a simple and fun taste test.

Detox and Re-energize	Are you feeling sluggish (or struggling to lose weight, experiencing aches and pains, digestive problems...)? Toxicity could well be the missing link.This talk covers: <ul><li>The new 'O' word which messes up your metabolism (as established by the scientists)</li><li>3 steps to detoxing for results</li><li>The ultimate detox shake recipe (so easy...)</li></ul>
1 in 3: cancer prevention strategies	More than 1 in 3 people in the UK will be diagnosed with cancer during their lifetime. However it's estimated at least 4 in 10 of these could be avoided if lifestyle changes were made at the right time. We share some steps you can start taking right now, to squeeze these 'modifiable' risk factors to an absolute minimum.
Take heart: 5 measures that will reduce cardiovascular risk now.	There are 7 Million people living with cardiovascular disease in the UK. Conditions which can be deadly, as well as sapping people's quality of life in and outside of work. In many cases, increased awareness and a few adjustments could prevent this from happening. We share 5 practical measures anyone can take now in order to beat heart disease and other related conditions. This talk can be complemented with individual arterial stiffness testing and personalised advice. We can produce a personalised report including vascular age, stiffness index and heart rate.
Stress Busting Special	Stress is estimated to account for 4 in 10 of all work related illnesses. Although it can have devastating effects, many struggle to understand what stress actually means, let alone how to deal with it. We explain in concrete terms how stress works in the body, how you can address its causes, and although stress can never be completely eliminated, how you can manage it and minimise its negative effects.

To discuss how you can get started in your organisation, get in touch with us.

Call 0203 598 4478 or email angela@superwellness.co.uk

References

1. Chowdhury R, et al. Association of Dietary, Circulating, and Supplement Fatty Acids With Coronary Risk: A Systematic Review and Meta-analysis. Ann Intern Med. 2014;160(6):398-406-406. doi: 10.7326/M13-1788

2. Gray J, et al. Eggs: Establishing the nutritional benefits. The Nutrition Bulletin 2013; 38(4): 438-449. doi: 10.1111/nbu.12066

3. Collins SM, Stress and the gastrointestinal tract IV. Modulation of intestinal inflammation by stress: basic mechanisms and clinical relevance. Am J Physiol. 2001;280:G315–G318.

4. McCance RA, Widdowson EM. A study on the mineral depletion of the foods available to us as a nation over the period 1940 to 1991.Medical Research Council 1991.

5. Schöttker B et al, Vitamin D and mortality: meta-analysis of individual participant data from a large consortium of cohort studies from Europe and the United States, BMJ, 17 June 2014. doi: 10.1136/bmj.g3656

6. Morck TA, Lynch SR, Cook JD. Inhibition of food iron absorption by coffee, Am J Clin Nutr. 1983 Mar; 37(3):416-20

7. Martin W et al, Dietary protein intake and renal function, Nutrition & Metabolism 2005, 2(25).doi:10.1186/1743-7075-2-25

8. Turnbaugh P, A core gut microbiome in obese and lean twins, Nature January 2009, 457, 480-484. doi:10.1038/nature07540

9. Arrieta MC, Alterations in intestinal permeability, Gut. Oct 2006 55(10): 1512–1520.doi:10.1136/gut.2005.085373

10. Dhurandar EJ, The effectiveness of breakfast recommendations on weight loss: a randomized controlled trial, Am J Clin Nutr. Jun 2014 4;100(2):507-513

11. Maki K, Acute Satiety Effects of Sausage/Egg-based Convenience Breakfast Meals in Premenopausal Women, presented at the Obesity Society's annual scientific meeting in Atlanta on Nov. 14, 2013.

12. Mamerow MM, Dietary Protein Distribution Positively Influences 24-h Muscle Protein Synthesis in Healthy Adults, Journal of Nutrition, 2014

13. Hounsome, N et al. Plant Metabolites and Nutritional Quality of Vegetables. Journal Food of Science. Vol.73, Nr. 4, p. 4862, 2008

14. Harvard Health Publications, Harvard Medical School, Abundance of fructose not good for the liver, heart, Sept 2011 (http://www.health.harvard.edu/newsletters)

15. Manuela PGM, Effect of capsaicin on substrate oxidation and weight maintenance after modest body-weight loss in human subjects. British Journal of Nutrition (2003), 90, 651–659 DOI: 10.1079/BJN2003938

16. Li Y, AMPK phosphorylates and inhibits SREBP activity to attenuate hepatic steatosis and atherosclerosis in diet-induced insulin-resistant mice, Cell Metab. 2011 Apr 6;13(4):376-88. doi: 10.1016/j.cmet.2011.03.009.

17. Schwalfenberg GK, The Alkaline Diet: Is There Evidence That an Alkaline pH Diet Benefits Health? Journal of Environmental and Public Health, 2012 (http://www.ncbi.nlm.nih.gov/pmc/articles/PMC3195546/)

18. Armstrong LE, Mild Dehydration Affects Mood in Healthy Young Women, J. Nutr. January 1, 2012 jn.111.142000 doi: 10.3945/jn.111.142000

19. Centers for Disease Control and Prevention – online factsheet Bisphenol A (BPA) http://www.cdc.gov/biomonitoring/BisphenolA_FactSheet.html

20. Weston A Price Foundation website. http://www.westonaprice.org/health-topics/living-with-phytic-acid/

21. The Nutrition Foundation. http://www.nutrition.org.uk/nutritionscience/nutrients/dietary-fibre

22. Anderson JW, Health benefits of dietary fiber. Nutr Rev. 2009 Apr;67(4):188-205. doi: 10.1111/j.1753-4887.2009.00189.x.

23. Ahmed S et al, Drug versus sweet reward: greater attraction to and preference for sweet versus drug cues. Addict Biol. 2014 Mar 7. doi: 10.1111/adb.12134.

24. Kulinski JP, Association Between Cardiorespiratory Fitness and Accelerometer-Derived Physical Activity and Sedentary Time in the General Population. Published Online: Mayo Clinic Proceedings. Volume 89, Issue 8, Pages 1063–1071. July 07, 2014. doi: http://dx.doi.org/10.1016/j.mayocp.2014.04.019

25. Thosar SS, Effect of Prolonged Sitting and Breaks in Sitting Time on Endothelial Function. Med Sci Sports Exerc. 2014 Aug 18.

26. DiPietro L, Three 15-min bouts of moderate postmeal walking significantly improves 24-h glycemic control in older people at risk for impaired glucose tolerance. Diabetes Care. 2013 Oct;36(10):3262-8. doi: 10.2337/dc13-0084.

27. McGuff D, Little J, Body by Science – a research based program for strength training, body building and complete fitness in 12 minutes a week. McGraw-Hill;1 edition (January 1, 2009) ISBN-10: 0071597174

28. Braden D, The Sprint 8 exercise protocol is a novel approach to fighting obesity efficiently among middle-aged females by substantially increasing GH serum levels naturally. King's Daughters Medical Center, University of Mississippi Medical Center, Copiah-Lincoln Community College, Wesson, MS, USA. June 2, 2012

29. Cornelis MC, Genome-Wide Meta-Analysis Identifies Regions on 7p21 (AHR) and 15q24 (CYP1A2) As Determinants of Habitual Caffeine Consumption, PLOS Genetics, April 07, 2011 doi: 10.1371/journal.pgen.1002033

30. Keller A, Does the perception that stress affects health matter? The association with health and mortality. Health Psychol. 2012 Sep;31(5):677-84. doi: 10.1037/a0026743.

31. Crum AJ, Rethinking stress: the role of mindsets in determining the stress response. J Pers Soc Psychol. 2013 Apr;104(4):716-33. doi: 10.1037/a0031201.

32. Ariga A, Brief and rare mental "breaks" keep you focused: deactivation and reactivation of task goals preempt vigilance decrements. Cognition. 2011 Mar;118(3):439-43. doi: 10.1016/j.cognition.2010.12.007

33. Kleitman N, Basic rest-activity cycle—22 years later. Sleep: Journal of Sleep Research & Sleep Medicine, Vol 5(4), Dec 1982, 311-317

34. Nawijn J, Vacationers Happier, but Most not Happier After a Holiday. Applied Research in Quality of Life, March 2010, Volume 5, Issue 1, pp 35-47

35. Jacobs TL, Self-reported mindfulness and cortisol during a Shamatha meditation retreat, Health Psychol. 2013 Oct;32(10):1104-9. doi: 10.1037/a0031362

36. Colantuoni C, Evidence That Intermittent, Excessive Sugar Intake Causes Endogenous Opioid Dependence, Obesity Research, Volume 10, Issue 6, pages 478–488, June 2002 DOI: 10.1038/oby.2002.66

37. Beunza GA, Alcohol intake, wine consumption and the development of depression: the PREDIMED study, BMC Med. 2013 Aug 30;11:192. doi: 10.1186/1741-7015-11-192.

38. Sears ME, Review Article: Arsenic, Cadmium, Lead, and Mercury in Sweat: A Systematic Review. Environ Public Health. 2012; 2012: 258968.

39. Cheung Y. Evening Blue-Enriched Light Exposure Increases Hunger and Alters Metabolism in Normal Weight Adults. Sleep. 2014

40. Donga E. A Single Night of Partial Sleep Deprivation Induces Insulin Resistance in Multiple Metabolic Pathways in Healthy Subjects. Journal of Clinical Endocrinology & Metabolism. 10.1210, 2009-2430. 2010

41. Maury E. Circadian Rhythms and Metabolic Syndrome: From Experimental Genetics to Human Disease. Circulation Research. 106, 447-462. 2010

42. Van Cauter E. Roles of Circadian Rhythmicity and Sleep in Human Glucose Metabolism. Endocrine Reviews. 18(5), 716-738. 1997

43. Humphries P. Direct and indirect cellular effects of aspartame on the brain. European Journal of Clinical Nutrition. 62, 451–462; 2008 doi: 10.1038/sj.ejcn.1602866;

RECIPE
SECTION

Recipes for Everyday Success

Do you need some inspiration to stick with a healthy lifestyle? This recipe book is designed specifically for time-starved high achievers who want to take control of their eating patterns, without giving up the day job. These tasty, nutritious, easy recipes for breakfast, lunch and dinner are divided into 2 categories to help you get organised:

 15 minutes
preparation or less

 Suitable for batch cooking
(longer preparation but lends itself to storing portions for later)

PLANNING AND PREPARATION

You'll find these recipes easy and enjoyable to make (as well as very tasty!), providing you set aside a bit of time for planning each week (as you get into the swing of things, you'll find the planning becomes second nature and may only even take a couple of minutes.)

Planning just means deciding which recipes you'll make and when (the batch cooking recipes lend themselves well to weekends), and drawing up a list of ingredients you'll be needing (see the ingredients list at the end of this book). It's also important to find the most effective way to get your supplies (buying online or in bulk is a huge time saver, as is getting organic veg boxes delivered to your home). **Check the recommended suppliers list online at www.superwellness.co.uk/eat-well-at-work/recommended-suppliers**

Whichever way you decide to do your shopping, once it's planned and done, you'll be more than 50% there already. Think of it as your 'mise en place' - professional chefs always lay out all of the ingredients they'll need for their shift, so they can work efficiently and achieve Michelin star results. In the same way, you can save huge amounts of time and effort by being prepared. And focus on optimum nutrition to help you be at your best.

CONTENTS

Breakfast

- ✗ Berry Oat Pancakes
- 🕘 Rye Bread with Ripe Avocado and Hot Smoked Salmon
- 🕘 Green Protein Smoothie
- 🕘 Protein Shake with Berries
- 🕘 Mushroom Tofu Scramble
- ✗ Mini Silken Tofu Frittatas

Lunch

- 🕘 Butterbean, Mackerel and Egg Salad
- 🕘 Mediterranean Omelette
- ✗ Moroccan Quinoa Salad
- 🕘 Fajita Wrap with Chicken Tikka and Avocado
- 🕘 Greek Salad Wrap

Dinner

- 🕐 Tandoori Salmon, Sweet Potato & Delicious Avocado Salsa
- 🕐 Cannellini Bean Dip
- ✖ Liver Loving Super Pasta
- 🕐 Hot Sweet & Sour Grilled Salmon with Shiitake Mushrooms
- ✖ Thai Green Chicken Curry
- ✖ Mulligatawny Soup
- 🕐 Black Bean Green Wraps
- ✖ Dhansak
- ✖ Quinoa Chapattis

Snacks

- ✖ Tahini and Chocolate Cake
- 🕐 Spicy Coco Winter Warmer

Shopping list

> **Whichever way you decide to do your shopping, once it's planned and done, you'll be more than 50% there already.**

Breakfast recipes

Berry Oat Pancakes

If you want a change from porridge, then look no further. This winner of a breakfast is like porridge in pancake form. It's satisfying and tastes fantastic.

Several of my clients now cook up a batch of these over the weekend, store them in the fridge and just warm them up on week days.

What a treat to start the day with!

Serves 2

INGREDIENTS

For the pancakes:

- 175g (6oz) oat flour (or blend whole oat flakes in a coffee grinder)
- 1 large free range egg
- 250 ml milk or substitute (Koko coconut milk, Ecomil almond milk or oat milk)
- A little coconut oil or (non extra virgin) olive oil for frying
- 1 tsp vanilla extract

For the topping:

- 300g blueberries, raspberries, blackberries or strawberries
- ½ tbsp xylitol (or 1 tsp muscovado sugar) to taste
- 2 tbsp low fat organic plain yoghurt

PREPARATION

1. Leave berries and xylitol (or sugar) to simmer with a splash of water until they soften
2. Whisk the pancake ingredients together to form a batter
3. Oil the frying pan and leave a minute on the hob to heat.
4. Ladle the batter in small amounts onto the frying pan to make small pancakes
5. Serve covered with the cooked blueberries and a tablespoon of yoghurt

Rye Bread with Ripe Avocado and Hot Smoked Salmon

You can use dark rye bread or German style pumpernickel bread for this breakfast recipe. Rye is dense and lower GL (glycaemic load) compared to other types of grain, it is also rich in insoluble fibre, which binds to toxins in the colon and helps remove them efficiently. Rye does contain gluten (although less than wheat) so if you are going gluten free, you could use the savoury topping from this recipe on the oat pancakes (using gluten free oats for the flour).

🕐 Serves 1

INGREDIENTS
- 1.5 pieces of German rye bread (you can also use wholemeal)
- 1 large ripe avocado
- 50g hot smoked salmon flakes
- Juice of half a lemon

PREPARATION

1. Roughly chop the ripe avocado and squash on to the bread with a fork.
2. Flake the salmon on top and squeeze lemon juice over the top.

Green Protein Smoothie

This green smoothie is a rich symphony of powerful nutrients that will feed and detoxify your whole body. Packed full of phyto-nutrients each bringing unique and subtle benefits, it works on many levels. Here are just a few of its key properties:

Cucumber and celery both have diuretic properties, helping to remove toxins from the body. Kiwis and limes are rich in vitamin C, a powerful antioxidant which counters the damaging effects of free radicals responsible for ageing and wrinkles.

Avocados are a powerhouse of essential fats, brilliant for preventing dry skin. They also contain large amounts of sterolins, a protein proven to reduce the appearance of age spots, scars and sun damage. The oil from avocados has been proven to increase the amount of collagen in the skin. According to the UCLA Center for Human Nutrition in California, compared to other fruits, avocados have the highest Vitamin E content - another powerful antioxidant which helps to keep the skin from oxidizing. Unusually for a non-fatty fruit, kiwis are also a great source of Vitamin E.

🕒 **Serves 1**

INGREDIENTS:
- 300ml spring or filtered water
- 80g Cucumber
- 80g Spinach
- 1 Kiwi
- 60g Celery
- 60g Avocado (approx half a large avocado)
- 15g pea protein (you can also use whey or other types of protein providing they are free of additives and sweeteners)
- Juice of half a lime
- Ingredients must be fresh, raw and preferably organic.

PREPARATION:
1. Make the smoothie fresh first thing each morning by placing the water in the blender first.
2. Chop all ingredients, add one at a time and blend until smooth with the protein powder
3. Divide the smoothie into two servings. Consume half before breakfast and and the second half before lunch, having kept it refrigerated or placed in a cold thermos flask.

Protein Shake with Berries

Having a protein breakfast is a smart move if you want to lose weight or better control your blood sugars - and appetite throughout the day. Especially if you struggle to eat or make time for breakfast first thing. One of the big reasons for this is that our blood sugars are naturally higher in the morning. Insulin release from the pancreas also follows a circadian rhythm, so carbohydrates consumed in the morning will lead to more fat storage than in the evening.

A note of caution: when choosing a protein powder, always check for additives and sweeteners (avoid any brands which contain maltodextrin or sucralose). Check my list of recommended suppliers at www.superwellness.co.uk/eat-well-at-work/recommended-suppliers

🕐 **Serves 1**

INGREDIENTS

- 50g Impact Whey Protein powder – Unflavoured (or other brand with no sweeteners or additives)
- 1 tablespoon Chia seeds
- Between 50 and 100g berries (blueberries, raspberries, strawberries, etc...)
- 1 large tumbler of Koko coconut milk (or unsweetened oat milk or almond milk)

PREPARATION
Mix all ingredients in a blender and drink.

Mushroom Tofu Scramble

A versatile breakfast or brunch recipe, which you can adapt to suit the ingredients you have in your fridge. You can use any type of mushroom you like – shiitake mushrooms are especially tasty, and renowned for their benefits. Not only are they a rich source of bio-available iron, and fantastic immune boosters, recent research has also shown they have protective properties when it comes to our blood vessels.

🕐 Serves 1

INGREDIENTS
- 100g Clearspring organic silken tofu (1/3 packet)
- 1 large organic free range egg
- 70g mushrooms
- 4 cherry tomatoes, chopped in two
- 1 handful spinach
- 2 tsp olive oil

PREPARATION

1. Oil the frying pan and add mushrooms over the heat.
2. Once the mushrooms have softened, add spinach and cherry tomatoes
3. While the spinach is wilting in the pan, take a bowl and mix the silken tofu with the egg.
4. Beat with a fork, then pour over the mushrooms, tomatoes and spinach.
5. Fold every now and again to ensure the tofu/egg mixture is cooked through (should take about 5 mins)

Mini Silken Tofu Frittatas

This is a tasty and fun brunch recipe, packed full of colourful plant nutrients (and there's nothing to stop you improvising with what you have in your veg basket! Cherry tomatoes, lightly steamed broccoli or asparagus – the sky is the limit!)

I also enjoy this because it's a lighter version of a traditional fully-egged frittata. The silken tofu is light and lends a gorgeous soft texture to the whole thing. Tofu is high in phyto-estrogens which help with hormone balancing (with tofu, you need to be sure to source good quality products rather than highly processed versions which unfortunately can turn soya beans into an unhealthy ingredient!)

You could make a simpler version of this by leaving the muffin tin in the cupboard and simply scrambling all the ingredients together in a frying pan. This is a perfect recipe if you're looking to lose weight – a high protein breakfast first thing really kicks your metabolism into action!

✗ **Makes 12 small frittatas (in a muffin tin)**

INGREDIENTS
- 300g Clearspring organic silken tofu (1 packet)
- 1 handful of baby spinach leaves

- 5 large organic free range eggs
- 12 pieces of sun drenched tomatoes
- 12 pieces of grilled artichoke in olive oil
- 100g chopped feta cheese
- 2 heaped teaspoons of mustard with seeds
- Pinch of sea salt
- Pinch of pepper
- 2 tsp olive oil

PREPARATION

1. Oil the muffin tin and heat the oven to 150 degrees
2. Lay a few leaves in each muffin space
3. Break the eggs into a bowl and use a fork to mix in the silken tofu, mustard, feta cheese and seasoning.
4. Spoon this mixture into the 12 muffin spaces, on top of the spinach leaves
5. Add the sun drenched tomatoes to 6 and the artichoke to the other 6.
6. Leave in the oven for 10 - 15 minutes

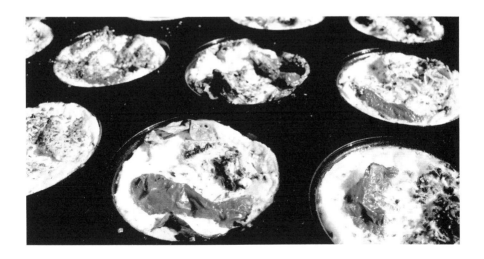

Butterbean, Mackerel and Egg Salad

Here's a satisfying packed lunch you can put together in 5 minutes. It's guaranteed to keep afternoon hunger pangs at bay, thanks to its ideal combo of ingredients rich in protein, beneficial fats and fibre. Butter beans have a delicate flavour and supply magnesium, which helps relax the arteries. One study found that those who ate legumes at least four times a week had a 22% lower risk of cardiovascular disease. They're an excellent source of protein as well as great fibre.

Several of my clients now cook up a batch of these over the weekend, store them in the fridge and just warm them up on week days.

Beans are also great for protecting the cells in your colon, because they contain 'resistant starch'. While most starches are broken down by enzymes in the small intestine into sugar, which is then absorbed into the blood, resistant starch makes its way to the colon, where it gets fermented by intestinal bacteria. This fermentation produces 'butyrate', a fatty acid which feeds the colon cells and may protect them against cancer.

A good reason to live a life full of beans!

✕🕐 Serves 1

INGREDIENTS

- ½ tin butter beans, drained and rinsed
- 1 small smoked mackerel fillet
- 1 hard-boiled egg
- 1 large handful rocket, watercress or salad leaves
- ½ ripe avocado
- 5 cherry tomatoes
- 2 spring onions
- 1 tablespoon extra virgin olive oil
- 1 capful of balsamic vinegar
- 1 pinch black pepper
- Optional: 1 fajita wrap

PREPARATION:

1. Chop the tomatoes, spring onions, egg and avocado and put them in a bowl.
2. Break up the mackerel fillet and add to the bowl together with the rinsed butter beans and salad leaves.
3. Drizzle with the olive oil and balsamic vinegar.
4. Serve in a bowl or in a wrap if on the move.

Mediterranean Omelette

Most days when I'm working from home, and wanting a quick but hot lunch, I opt for a tasty omelette. The sun drenched tomatoes add a lovely sharpness as well as a whole army of antioxidants, including vitamin C and carotenoids to support your immune system. Lycopene is one of these carotenoids, and is known in particular for its benefits in lowering the risk of prostate cancer.

🕐 Serves 1

INGREDIENTS
- 2 large free range organic eggs
- 8 pieces of sun drenched tomato
- 50g feta cheese, chopped
- 1 tsp mixed herbs (and fresh if you wish)
- 2 tsp olive oil (cooking)

PREPARATION
1. Oil a frying pan and add the feta cheese and sun drenched tomatoes
2. Mix the eggs in a bowl, and once the feta cheese has begun to melt, pour the eggs on top
3. Once the eggs have started to cook, sprinkle the herbs on top.
4. Fold to allow the omelette to cook through

Moroccan Quinoa Salad

A supernutritious take on the original sun-packed 'Tabbouleh', this recipe lends itself well to making in large amounts and keeping in the fridge for Tupperware refills. It packs a punch in both the protein and plant antioxidant departments, making it the perfect low glycaemic load meal.

Quinoa is a 'superfood' grown in the Peruvian Andes, more akin to a seed than a grain. It is a very useful substitute for couscous as it's so high in protein (instead of higher glycaemic load carbohydrates), avoids the wheat couscous is made from (which causes digestive problems in many) and is a true powerhouse of vitamins and minerals (whilst couscous is comparatively nutritionally poor).

Serves 1

INGREDIENTS

- 50g quinoa cooked with 1/2 tsp turmeric and 1/2 tsp bouillon powder (you can prepare a big batch in advance and freeze 50g portions)
- ¼ tin chick peas, drained and rinsed
- 1 small sized pepper
- ½ a chilli (optional)
- 5 cherry tomatoes
- 2 inch section of cucumber
- Handful of parsley
- 50g feta cheese, diced.

- 2 or 3 mint leaves
- 1 tablespoon extra virgin olive oil
- Juice of half a lemon

PREPARATION
Quinoa: cook a whole packet in one go, and freeze 50g portions
Quinoa is not only a complete protein (containing all of the
essential amino acids), it is also an incredibly rich source of
vitamins and minerals.
Simmer in some water with an added teaspoon of turmeric and
Swiss vegetable bouillon powder. Cooking time is approx 10-12
minutes. Keep checking to avoid overcooking. The seeds should
still be slightly chewy but not hard.

The Salad:
1. Chop the pepper, chilli, tomatoes, cucumber and parsley finely.
2. Add to a bowl with the cooked quinoa and drained chickpeas.
3. Chop the mint extra fine and mix in.
4. Drizzle with the olive oil and lemon.

Fajita Wrap with Chicken Tikka and Avocado

You can simply buy the ingredients for this recipe and assemble them at work. No lengthy preparation needed! For those avoiding wheat, this would work well as a salad too.

 Serves 1

INGREDIENTS
- 100g Tikka chicken breast chunks
- 1 ripe avocado (small)
- 3 cherry tomatoes
- 1 large handful rocket, watercress or salad leaves
- 2 tbsp plain organic yoghurt
- 1 clove garlic
- 2 or 3 mint leaves
- 1 tbsp lemon juice
- 1 fajita wrap

PREPARATION

1. In a small bowl, crush garlic into the yoghurt and mix with finely chopped mint.
2. Chop the tomatoes and avocado and put them in a separate bowl.
3. Add the chicken breast chunks, and mix everything with the yoghurt.
4. Empty the mix onto a wrap, with the handful of salad leaves, drizzle with lemon juice and fold ready for lunch.

Greek Salad Wrap

Greek salad is a classic recipe, and here I've jazzed it up with a mouthwatering hummus dressing. A great way of adding some more protein to the whole combo!

🕒 **Serves 1**

INGREDIENTS
- 100g Feta cheese, cubed
- 1 ripe avocado (small)
- 5 cherry tomatoes
- 1 small red onion
- 1 handful olives
- 1 large handful rocket, watercress or salad leaves
- 60g hummus
- 1 tbsp olive oil
- Juice of half a lemon
- 1 tbsp lemon juice
- 1 fajita wrap

PREPARATION

1. In a small bowl, mix hummus, olive oil and lemon juice to make a thick dressing.
2. Chop the tomatoes, onion and avocado and put them in a separate bowl.
3. Add the feta cheese, olives and salad leaves, and mix everything with the humus dressing.
4. Empty the mix onto a wrap, and fold ready for lunch (you can also increase the quantities of salad and remove the wrap).

Dinner recipes

Tandoori Salmon, Sweet Potato and Delicious Avocado Salsa

This well balanced dinner is a feast for the eyes and palate. Sweet potatoes are extremely high in beta-carotene, which the body can convert to vitamin A, beneficial for healthy skin, eyes and bones. As a fat soluble vitamin, it will be even better absorbed if eaten along with good fats. Just as well then that this meal has them in abundance: omega 3 containing salmon (in higher doses if you choose wild salmon), and oleic acid from olive oil and avocado. Great for your brain too! Oleic acid is one of the most common fats used in the myelin sheath, the envelope which protects the neurons.

🕒 Serves 2

INGREDIENTS:
- Salmon (you can also substitute chicken)
- 1 tsp curry powder
- 1 tbsp low fat plain yoghurt

- 2 wild salmon fillets
- 1 or 2 cloves of garlic, crushed
- 1 large sweet potato (or 2 small)

Salsa
- 1 ripe avocado
- 1 handful of cherry tomatoes (or 2 medium sized)
- 1 small red onion
- 1 fresh chilli
- 1 tbsp olive oil
- Juice of half a lemon
- 2 lemon wedges

PREPARATION:
1. Mix the curry powder in a bowl with the crushed garlic and yoghurt.
2. Cut the salmon into large chunks and leave it to marinade in the yoghurt and currymix for a minimum of 20 minutes.
3. Pop the sweet potato in the oven in its skin
4. Chop the salsa ingredients finely and mix together with olive oil.
5. When the sweet potato is cooked, pop the salmon chunks under the grill and rotate until grilled on both sides (5 minutes).
6. Serve with half the sweet potato and salsa sauce, with a wedge of lemon on the side

Cannellini Bean Dip

Potato mash, move over! This low glycaemic alternative certainly won't have you falling asleep over your keyboard. And if you ever get bored of hummus, this is a great option for dipping your crudités in. This close cousin to the kidney bean has a smooth, delicate and nutty flavour.

✖ 🕒 Serves 2, as a side, or as a dip

INGREDIENTS:
- 1 tin of cannellini beans, rinsed and drained
- 1 clove of garlic
- 1 tablespoon olive oil
- 1 teaspoon Swiss Bouillon Powder
- Juice of half a lemon
- 3 tablespoons of organic milk (or substitute with coconut, almond or oat milk)

PREPARATION:
1. Combine all of the ingredients together in a food processor, process for around 1 minute – et voila!
2. Warm up for a side of mash, or serve cold as a dip with crudités or oatcakes.

Liver Loving Super Pasta

Pure comfort on a plate, ready in 12 minutes, and comes with 'WOW!' taste factor guarantee. Wild rocket is considered a bitter food, and as such it stimulates bile flow out of the liver (helping it to detoxify). Part of the 'brassica' family, like broccoli, rocket contains many phytochemicals, including an 'indole' known to help detoxify hormones via the liver (it has been found to counter the carcinogenic effects of oestrogen).

As for artichokes, they are a natural liver tonic. Containing the phytonutrients Cynarine and Silymarin known to boost the regeneration of liver cells, they have long been considered a good natural remedy for hepatitis.

INGREDIENTS (PER PERSON):
- 2 small handfuls wholemeal pasta (or gluten free – seen here)
- ¼ tsp Chilli flakes
- 1 clove of garlic
- 1 small pinch Himalayan crystal salt
- 2 handfuls of Rocket
- 4-5 pieces of grilled Artichoke in olive oil, chopped (you can usually find these pre-prepared in the deli, or you can use fresh artichoke, which requires a bit more preparation time as you will need to steam it first)

- Alternatively you can use sun drenched tomatoes too
- 50g Halloumi cheese, diced
- 1 tablespoon pine nuts, grilled lightly
- 1 tablespoon olive oil (for cooking)

PREPARATION:
1. Add pasta to boiling water in a pan.
2. Meanwhile: Make a generous bed of rocket in a pasta bowl, add chopped artichokes.
3. Grill the Halloumi pieces till they just start to turn brown. Then lightly grill the pine-nuts (you can use a dry frying pan – no oil)
4. Once the pasta is cooked (keep testing to catch 'al dente'), drain and place the empty pan back on the gas. Add olive oil, chilli flakes and the garlic. Before the garlic starts to turn brown, add the cooked pasta and toss so that it's coated with the olive oil, chilli and garlic. Add a small pinch of salt.
5. Lay the pasta on top of the green bed of leaves and artichokes, place Halloumi cubes and sprinkle the pine nuts over the top before serving.

Hot Sweet and Sour Grilled Salmon with Shiitake Mushrooms

This is a great lean protein meal, high in essential fats and plant nutrients. Beta glucans from the shiitake mushrooms provide powerful immune boosting properties, as does allicin from the garlic, with its antibacterial benefits. Not to mention ginger, rich in gingerols, its active components shown to have cancer fighting credentials.

🕒 **Serves 2**

INGREDIENTS
- 1 punnet shiitake mushrooms
- 2 fillets wild salmon (farmed salmon is very low in omega 3s and poor quality)
- Juice of half a lemon
- Pinch of chilli flakes
- 2 tsp chopped ginger
- Crushed clove of garlic
- ½ tsp runny honey
- 2 tablespoons soy sauce or tamari sauce

PREPARATION:

1. Mix all of the ingredients apart from the salmon and the mushrooms in a bowl, then add the salmon and leave to marinate for at least 20 minutes.
2. Remove the salmon and grill until the skin goes crisp.
3. Meanwhile chop up the mushrooms and add other vegetables of your choice (e.g. peppers, courgettes, sugar snap peas, etc..). Stir fry for a couple of minutes, then add the rest of the marinade a couple of minutes before the vegetables are ready
4. Serve and enjoy!

Thai Green Chicken Curry

When I began making this recipe, years ago, I always stuck to the same vegetables (it had to be green beans, butternut squash and shitake mushrooms!). Then I started receiving a weekly organic box full of wonderful seasonal vegetables which I didn't have time to think up recipes for.

So I became more flexible and experimented with whatever was available in the kitchen – sweet potatoes,

Jerusalem artichokes (fantastic combo), cauliflower, you name it! I always try to keep a couple of portions of this green curry paste in the freezer so that all I have to do is throw everything in (10 minutes maximum including chopping time) and wait for it to cook (not that long depending how big the vegetable chunks are). And within half an hour, there's a beautifully fragrant nutritious home-made Thai curry on the table. This has been a firm favourite for quite a few years now!

INGREDIENTS

Curry paste

- (Enough for 3 batches of paste, which you can freeze, each providing 4 servings)
- 15 shallots
- 10 garlic cloves
- 3 Thai green chillies (or more to taste)
- 1 small bunch coriander
- 3 lemongrass stalks
- 1 tablespoon chopped ginger
- 2 teaspoons galangal paste (optional)

Sauce and contents

- Olive or coconut oil for cooking the paste
- 1 tin coconut milk
- 1 tsp Swiss vegetable bouillon powder
- 1 tsp Turmeric (optional)
- Your choice of seasonal vegetables
- Protein: Meat / Fish / Tempeh / Tofu / Grilled cashew nuts
- Kaffir lime leaves (optional)
- 1 tbsp Soy sauce or tamari sauce (increase to taste)
- 1 tbsp Fish sauce (optional),
- The juice of half a lime
- 3 drops Sesame oil (optional

PREPARATION

Curry paste:
1. Blend all ingredients together in a food processor to make 3 batches, each enough for four people.
2. Store extra portions of paste in the freezer (using small freezer bages, Tupperware boxes, or even disposable ice-cube bags)

Preparing the curry:
1. Stir fry the paste in olive oil or coconut oil on medium heat for 2 minutes
2. Heat 250 ml water in a kettle whilst adding the coconut milk and bouillon powder to the paste. Stir well, add the water and a few kaffir lime leaves (if available) and tsp turmeric (optional)
3. Add vegetables / tempeh / tofu / fish / meat etc... (add those which need the longest cooking time first, then keep checking until all ingredients are done but not overcooked)
4. When the curry is nearly ready, add a tablespoon of soy sauce or tamari sauce, fish sauce (optional), the juice of half a lime and some sesame oil (optional). Serve with brown rice or quinoa.

Mulligatawny Soup

This soup is one of my staple recipes at home. It's so quick to make a big batch of it, and so tasty too!

It's a great low glycaemic soup, high in proteins from the lentils (as high as 26%), with great fructo-oligosaccharides from the leeks and onions – and jerusalem artichokes if they are in there too (they help feed the beneficial bacteria in your gut). And spices... well they are always therapeutic in so many ways. Turmeric is particularly good as a powerful anti-inflammatory compound.

Mixed in with some goat's yoghurt or feta cheese, this can be a stand alone light meal, just perfect to warm you up on a cold winter's day!

INGREDIENTS
- Coconut oil or olive oil
- 3 large onions chopped
- 3 or 4 leeks, chopped, or 700g unpeeled courgettes, cut into 1 inch cubes or
- 2 sweet potatoes, peeled and cut into 1 inch cubes
- 225g tomatoes, skinned and chopped
- 4 handfuls of lentils (green and yellow work well but any will do), rinsed thoroughly (and even better, soaked for a few hours)
- 1 inch fresh ginger root, chopped
- 10 cardamom pods, seeds only
- 1 teaspoon cumin seeds
- 1 teaspoon fennel seeds
- 1 dessertspoon coriander seeds

- 2 teaspoons turmeric
- Sprinkle of chilli flakes to taste
- Pinch of sea salt
- 1 litre (or more) boiling water with 2 teaspoons Marigold Swiss Bouillon powder
- Juice of 1 lemon
- Goat's milk yoghurt

PREPARATION

1. First, heat the oil in a large soup pan, then add the onions and cook until they're a golden brown colour, then add the chopped ginger. Meanwhile place the cardamom, cumin and fennel seeds in a small frying pan to dry roast – this will take 2-3 minutes. As soon as the seeds start to jump, tip them into a coffee grinder and grind them finely, then add them to the onions along with the chilli flakes and turmeric. Now add the vegetables and lentils (you can also improvise with other vegetables if you wish). Season, then let the vegetables cook gently, covered– for about 10 minutes.
2. Add the water and bouillon powder and finish cooking gently until the lentils and vegetables are soft.
3. Roughly blend, leaving chunks of vegetables in the soup if you wish. Squeeze in the lemon juice and mix in.
4. Serve with a tablespoon of goat's yoghurt.

Mexican Power Bean Wraps

What a great way to end the day with this protein packed plant based meal! It combines the comfort factor from the black beans with the high nutrient value of raw plants. When you eat plants raw, you avoid destroying the flavonoids they contain. Flavonoids are plant pigments with anti-inflammatory, immune promoting benefits, which can often be destroyed in the cooking process (you can usually see the colour leeching away into the water used for boiling and even steaming vegetables). It's always a good idea to include some raw plant foods as part of every meal.

One plant compound which is particularly high in this recipe is capsaicin, the active ingredient in chillies. Capsaicin is a potent inhibitor of substance P, a neuropeptide associated with inflammation. The hotter the chilli, the more capsaicin it contains...

🕐 Serves 2

INGREDIENTS
Black bean filling
- 2 cans black beans, drained and rinsed
- 1 clove garlic
- 1 tsp cumin

- 2tsp ground coriander
- ½ tsp cayenne pepper
- 1 heaped tsp Swiss Bouillon powder
- Handful fresh coriander
- Olive oil
- Cos lettuce leaves for the wraps (alternatively, you can also use one Fajita wrap per person)

Salsa
- 1 ripe avocado
- Handful cherry tomatoes
- 1 small red onion
- 1 green chilli
- ½ lime, squeezed
- Olive oil
- Fresh coriander

PREPARATION
1. Put all the filling ingredients into a food processor and process roughly. Heat in a pan.
2. Chop salsa ingredients very fine.
3. Serve in a wrap with jalapeno chillies and crumbled feta cheese.

Dhansak

Who said healthy eating should be dull? This nutritious spicy dish lends itself beautifully to meat, prawns or vegetarian sources of protein.

It combines the comfort factor with a fantastic array of nutrients from vegetables of all colours, as well as a good combination of great quality protein and low GL carbohydrate foods.

You'll need to set a bit more time aside for this recipe (perhaps one for a relaxed Sunday afternoon) as it requires a bit of preparation. The result will be well worth it, as this large batch of food can save you precious time during the week, filling your freezer with handy portions of comforting bliss.

✕ Serves 6-8 people

INGREDIENTS

Spices:
- 2 teaspoons (tsp) of black peppercorns
- 3 tsp coriander seeds
- 1 tsp cumin seeds
- The seeds from 10 cardamom pods (discard the husks)
- ½ tsp turmeric
- 1 tsp ground fenugreek
- ½ chilli flakes (adjust for strength)

Other ingredients:
- 1 tablespoon (tbsp) coconut oil
- 2 onions, diced
- 4 cloves garlic, puréed
- 4 green chillies, sliced along the middle
- 1 inch piece of ginger, chopped finely
- 1x400g /14oz tin chopped tomatoes
- 4 fresh tomatoes, chopped
- 2 small sweet potatoes, cubed (alternatively you can use butternut squash, pumpkin or Jerusalem artichokes)
- ½ cauliflower (and/or 1 courgette and/or a handful of okra)
- 75g chard (or spinach, or kale, or chard)
- 150g/5 ½ oz red lentils, soaked for at least 1 hour, rinsed thoroughly and drained.
- Juice of 1 lime
- Handful of coriander leaves
- Your choice of vegetables: courgettes, okra

- Your choice of protein: chicken, lamb, beef, prawns, or vegetarian options such as tofu, tempeh or cashew nuts lightly roasted in the oven.

To serve
- Goat's, sheep's or soya yoghurt

PREPARATION

1. For the spice mix, heat a frying pan over a medium heat. Add the peppercorns, coriander seeds, cumin seeds and cardamom seeds and dry fry for 2-3 minutes or until fragrant.
2. Transfer them to a coffee grinder and grind to a powder.
3. Meanwhile, heat the coconut oil in a large cooking pot over a low heat, add the onion, chilli, ginger and garlic last of all. Fry gently until the onions have caramelized.
4. Add the tomatoes and the spice mix and cover with boiling water. Give the mixture a stir.
5. Add the soaked and drained lentils.
6. Add the vegetables (start with those which will require the most time – e.g. sweet potatoes and cauliflower – add leaves last so they don't overcook and dissolve).
7. Add your choice of protein (if it's meat, add it from the start, if it's prawns, tempeh or tofu, just 5 minutes from serving so they don't overcook, if you're serving with cashew nuts, you can add these separately when you serve the dhansak to keep them nice and crunchy.
8. Simmer until the lentils are soft. Add lime juice.
9. Serve with some chopped coriander on top and yoghurt on the side.

Quinoa Chapattis

Agreat alternative to wheat flour chapattis, these delicious Indian breads are beneficial in many ways. They manage to avoid gluten, which many are intolerant to, as well as boosting protein levels and offering a lower GL option to those wanting to fight cravings and lose weight.

✗ **Makes 6 chapattis**

INGREDIENTS
- 8 tablespoons quinoa flour, plus some extra for rolling
- 2 or 3 tablespoons goat's, sheep's or soya yoghurt (adjust as necessary)
- Coconut oil

PREPARATION
1. Mix the flour and yoghurt together to form a dough (adjust quantities as necessary to get a good consistency, not too sticky and not too dry).
2. Meanwhile place a flat bottomed pan with a thick base on the heat, with a dollop of coconut oil. Spread the oil evenly as it melts.
3. Knead the dough for a couple of minutes and split into 6 small balls.
4. Sprinkle your work surface with the extra quinoa flour and roll out the balls into 3 mm thick chapattis.
5. Fry 2 or 3 at a time on both sides and they are ready to serve.

Tahini and Chocolate Cake

This wonderful guilt-free cake has become a classic in our house as well as for many of my clients. Gluten free and low GL, it's also protein rich. Oh and it takes 15 minutes to make – tops!

Dark chocolate is packed with protective antioxidants and magnesium (a mineral which relaxes muscles and blood vessels). Tahini is packed with zinc, a mineral involved in over 200 functions in the body (and very helpful in skin conditions among many others). Quinoa flour is a great alternative to wheat flour, and much more protein rich. It's available online or in good health food shops, however if you're struggling to find it, you can also use an alternative like oat flour, or gluten free flour. Nuts add more protein to the mix, and hazelnuts in particular are one of the richest sources of vitamin E, a powerful antioxidant which protects your cell membranes from free radical damage (no wonder they are good for the skin!)

INGREDIENTS
- 4 large eggs
- 150 g dark chocolate (minimum 70%)
- 4 heaped tablespoons tahini paste (80g)

- ½ cup light muscovado sugar (or xylitol) (60g)
- 2 tablespoons quinoa flour
- 2 handfuls hazelnuts (or other nuts)
- Pinch of sea salt

PREPARATION

1. Preheat the oven to 180° C and butter a cake tin. Set aside.
2. In a separate tin, roast the hazelnuts until they start to turn slightly brown
3. Place the chocolate and tahini in a bain marie (in a bowl over simmering water) until melted
4. In a bowl, mix the eggs with the sugar and salt. Beat until pale in color and the volume of the batter has doubled.
5. Fold in gently the quinoa flour and the chocolate mix.
6. Add the roasted hazelnuts
7. Pour into the cake tin
8. Bake for 10-12 minutes

Spicy Coco Winter Warmer

This is a perfect snack for the evening, especially if you have a long gap between dinner and bedtime. Almonds contain tryptophan, an amino acid which gets converted into serotonin, a sleep inducing brain chemical. They also contain magnesium, a mineral known for its muscle relaxant properties. Cardamom has a reputation for being a sedative spice, and cinnamon helps balance blood sugars, avoiding the lows which often wake people up in the middle of the night.

🕑 Serves 1

INGREDIENTS
- 1 Mug of Koko coconut milk (Ecomil Almond milk or oat milk will work as well)
- 1 heaped teaspoon of raw or 100% cacao (no added sugar)
- Ground almonds (or unflavoured protein powder)
- ½ teaspoon ground cinnamon
- 3 cardamom pods, hulled
- 3 cloves

Warm up, serve!

Your Shopping List

FROM THE HEALTH FOOD SHOP / ONLINE

- ☐ Almond butter
- ☐ Chia seeds
- ☐ Quinoa
- ☐ Quinoa flour
- ☐ Oat flour (you can also grind whole oats in the coffee grinder)
- ☐ Protein powder (whey, pea, hemp or other – unflavoured)
- ☐ Coconut oil (organic)
- ☐ Himalayan crystal salt (and grinder)
- ☐ Frozen berries
- ☐ Tahini paste
- ☐ Tempeh (especially vegetarians)
- ☐ Tofu
- ☐ Xylitol sweetener

STAPLES FROM THE SUPERMARKET

- ☐ Olive oil for cooking (not extra virgin)
- ☐ Extra virgin olive oil (for salads)
- ☐ Balsamic vinegar
- ☐ Nairn's oatcakes
- ☐ Rye bread
- ☐ Silken tofu (Clearspring or other brand)
- ☐ Koko coconut milk or Almond milk (Ecomil)
- ☐ Or oat milk
- ☐ Thick coconut milk (for use in curries)
- ☐ Wholemeal pasta or gluten free
- ☐ Porridge oats (rolled oats)
- ☐ Raw unsalted nuts: almonds, walnuts, hazelnuts, brazil nuts, cashew nuts

- ☐ Red lentils
- ☐ Fajita wraps
- ☐ Honey
- ☐ Vanilla extract

- ☐ Soy sauce or tamari sauce
- ☐ Galangal paste (optional)
- ☐ Kaffir lime leaves (optional)
- ☐ Fish sauce (optional)
- ☐ Sesame oil (optional)
- ☐ Pine nuts
- ☐ 100% cocoa powder
- ☐ Swiss Vegetable Bouillon powder

- ☐ Tinned pulses: butter beans, chick peas, cannellini beans, black beans
- ☐ Tinned tomatoes

SPICES:
- ☐ Cayenne pepper
- ☐ Cardamom pods
- ☐ Chilli flakes
- ☐ Cloves
- ☐ Cumin – ground and seeds

- ☐ Coriander – ground and seeds
- ☐ Curry powder
- ☐ Fennel seeds
- ☐ Ground turmeric
- ☐ Ground fenugreek
- ☐ Ground cinnamon
- ☐ Mixed herbs
- ☐ Peppercorns

FRESH FROM THE SUPERMARKET

- ☐ Peppers
- ☐ Chilli
- ☐ Tomatoes
- ☐ Cucumber
- ☐ Spring onions
- ☐ Red onions
- ☐ Bag of rocket, watercress or salad leaves (organic)
- ☐ Ripe avocadoes

- ☐ Sugar snap peas
- ☐ Parsley
- ☐ Mint
- ☐ Coriander
- ☐ Garlic
- ☐ Ginger
- ☐ Fresh chillies
- ☐ Lemongrass
- ☐ Mushrooms (shiitake or other)
- ☐ Other seasonal veggies (sweet potatoes, Jerusalem artichokes, leeks, broccoli, courgettes, spinach, asparagus, etc..)
- ☐ Lemons
- ☐ Limes
- ☐ Other seasonal fruit (to have with nuts)

- ☐ Free range organic eggs

- ☐ Olives

- ☐ Sun drenched tomatoes
- ☐ Grilled artichokes in olive oil
- ☐ Humus (organic and / or mini pots)
- ☐ Feta cheese (or goat's cheese)
- ☐ Low fat plain yoghurt (preferably goat's or sheep's)
- ☐ Halloumi (for grilling)

- ☐ Wild salmon fillets
- ☐ Hot smoked salmon
- ☐ Smoked mackerel fillets

NOTES:

14438659R00142

Printed in Great Britain
by Amazon.co.uk, Ltd.,
Marston Gate.